The No-Regrets
BUCKET LIST

Dedication

This book is dedicated to the wonderful
people in my life who support me with
love, guidance and wisdom.

And to my daughter, Angela, who has made
me realize how important it is to create the
kind of legacy you want to leave behind.

The Wise Woman
COLLECTION

The No-Regrets
BUCKET LIST

The No-Regrets
BUCKET LIST

THIS BOOK IS A GIFT

FROM: *MARION*

TO: *KAILA*

To No Regrets!

Marion

The Wise Woman
COLLECTION ™

The No-Regrets
BUCKET LIST

Living the Life You
Were Meant to Live

Marion Elizabeth Witte

WISE OWL
PUBLISHING INC.

Ventura, California

Wise Woman Collection – The No-Regrets Bucket List

Wise Owl Publishing, Inc.
Ventura, California

Cover and book design by Mark Sherman Brand Development
Printed in the United States of America

Copyright @ 2013 by Marion Elizabeth Witte

LCCN 2012951828
ISBN-13: 978-0-9882411-1-4 (print)
ISBN-13: 978-0-9882411-4-5 (electronic book)

Publisher's Cataloging-in-Publication

Witte, Marion Elizabeth.
The wise woman collection - The No-Regrets Bucket List:
Living the Life You Were Meant to Live / Marion Elizabeth Witte.
p. cm.
LCCN 2012951828
ISBN 9780988241114
ISBN 9780988241145

1. Self-actualization (Psychology) 2. Women--Conduct
of life. I. Title. II. Title: No-regrets bucket list.

BF637.S4W58 2013 158.1'082
QBI12-600231

THE NO-REGRETS BUCKET LIST

Contents

Author's Note

I recently experienced a major health scare which resulted in my hospitalization and ensuing recuperation at home. I frequently joke about how "each of us has a big bus waiting to take us out of this life." As I reflected on what I had faced, and the possibility of a very different outcome, I came to fully understand the undeniable truth in my anecdote. While lying quietly in my hospital bed, I had time to contemplate my life and whether I had achieved the life goals I set out for myself. The answer I found myself responding with was "No."

While some of the uncompleted tasks I contemplated are secondary to my primary goal of living a meaningful life, others remain a significant part of what I want to accomplish. I now understand there is no time like the present to complete my unfinished business.

And so, I came up with the concept of a No-Regrets Bucket List, which I developed for my personal use. This book is the outcome of the process I undertook to examine my life and to determine the legacy I want to leave.

The information in this book is based on my personal observations and experiences, and the wise counsel offered to me by many others. I hope the reader will find something useful in these pages, as I believe we can benefit from what others have learned, since we are all a "work-in-progress."

Blessings,
  Marion Witte

VI

Foreword

Why Create A No-Regrets Bucket List?

There are literally thousands of books available that address the goals of attracting love, achieving financial success and finding happiness, and those publications can be valuable resources for individuals working towards those objectives.

This book addresses the concept of achieving our ultimate goal in life – living a meaningful life and leaving a legacy of which we are proud. The concept behind the No-Regrets Bucket List suggests that there is a need to determine who we want to be during our lifetime and that the creation of guidelines can assist us in that process.

The chapters in this book provide a sampling of ideas the reader might consider for inclusion on their own no-regrets bucket list. Since life goals are highly personal, any list created would obviously be unique and specific to the individual and their circumstances. The intention of this book is to have the reader consider concepts they might not have previously contemplated, and which may form the foundation for taking action in an specific area, so there are no regrets in the future about not doing so.

This book is intended to encourage everyone to live the life they came here to live with no regrets at its end. This can be accomplished if we sit in the driver's seat of our life, take charge of our dreams, and create the type of life we want and the way we want to be remembered.

Since we are all going to be but a memory someday, let's make it the best one it can be.

Live a Life of No Regrets

"Life is short, break the rules. Forgive quickly, kiss slowly.
Love truly, laugh uncontrollably.
And never regret anything that makes you smile."

~Mark Twain

A life of purpose cannot be defined by a singular accomplishment. Each person has a unique combination of gifts and abilities that make up their contribution to the world. I highly encourage reaching for the stars, but you don't have to be a Pulitzer Prize winner to leave a legacy. Leaving a legacy and living a life with no regrets is more about embracing the lessons life teaches. It is about having the wisdom to grow, learn, expand and change when needed.

So what exactly is a legacy?
A legacy is what you leave behind for the world to remember. It can be the influence you had on a friend or the job you performed as a parent. It can be a charitable contribution or the impact you made on the business world. Large or small, we are all leaving a legacy. Living a life with no regrets involves defining that legacy. You must create it yourself, for only you know what type of life you want to lead. It is never too late to leave a mark, even if it is as simple as a smile or a kind word for those around you. Many times we underestimate the impact of a small gesture. Kind expressions, no matter how seemingly insignificant, may be the thing that people remember about you after your time has passed.

How to live with no regrets

Living a life free of regrets involves letting go. It involves letting go of the would-have, should-have, could-have mentality. Dwelling on how you could have lived differently is detrimental to your spirit. Sometimes we do the best we can with the knowledge we have at the time. Frequently the wrong choices bring us to the right places. Make the choice now to forgive yourself, as the world needs the best of you. You cannot give your best when you dwell on past hurts or perceived mistakes.

Another part of leaving a legacy is living a full life that you love and which you are sharing with others. Ask yourself the following questions:

- What have I enjoyed most in my life so far?
- What am I passionate about?
- What would I like to be remembered for?

Questions like these can be powerful in defining your goals and moving you into a life that you are proud to live.

To live a life with no regrets and leave behind a legacy for your family and the world, begin by simply enjoying your life on a daily basis. Forgive yourself and others, follow your own path, seek happiness in the little things, and find something you enjoy that allows you to share and give back. Be kind and gracious to those you meet and embrace the joyful life you were meant to live.

As Benjamin Disraeli said, "Man is only truly great when he acts from his passions."

Live out your passions and rest assured that you can leave this life with no regrets.

"Get correct views of life, and learn to see the world in its true light. It will enable you to live pleasantly, to do good and when summoned away, to leave without regret."

~Robert E. Lee

Chapter 1

Discover The Real You

"To be yourself in a world that is constantly trying to make you something else is the greatest accomplishment."

~Ralph Waldo Emerson

Accept What You Can't Change

"Do what you can, with what you have, where you are."

~Theodore Roosevelt

*W*e all have circumstances or people in our lives that we wish we could change. Ask yourself these questions: What would you change about your appearance? What societal problems do you complain about? What family members, individuals or groups bother you? If you experienced a negative thought or feeling in response to these questions, you may be experiencing resistance and not accepting what you can't change. The answers to these questions may also give you clues about some deeply-held beliefs which you may need to challenge.

Is life really in the struggle?

It's been said that there is life in the struggle. But isn't there more life and more happiness in a peaceful, harmonious existence? Western culture predominantly views life as a battle that must be fought. We struggle with our weight; we battle to get ahead financially; we confront political opponents; and we feel we must fight for a cause. And certainly there is a time to stand up and fight. But after a while this behavior becomes habitual and ingrained in our psyche. We find ourselves weary from constantly warring against factions that are largely out of our control. Worse yet, our happiness and peace of mind become compromised in the process. The resulting state of being can be likened to a hamster on a wheel engaged in a nonproductive and vicious cycle that is defined by opposition and resistance. It never occurs to us, instead of trying to battle or confront every issue, that maybe we need to learn acceptance.

What is acceptance?

Our society has come to view acceptance as a passive act - a sign of resignation, failure, or giving up. It's not. Rather, acceptance is being able to recognize and embrace a situation by consciously acknowledging it without judgment or criticism. Acceptance is a far cry from doing nothing. In fact, by welcoming an accepting attitude, you begin to simplify your inner environment and eliminate the focus on resistance. Being able to come to terms with and accept what cannot be changed enables us to allow space for clearer thoughts and, ultimately, more effective action.

Non-acceptance can lead to pain and sorrow

It may seem to go against common sense on the surface, but in the face of things that do not or will not change, we still have a choice - our reaction. No matter what kind of structure we create in our lives in an attempt to maintain control, there will be those elements that fall outside of our preset parameters. People many times won't behave like we would want them to act. There will always be sickness, natural disasters, poverty, political unrest, and death. If we do not have the psychological tools in place to handle unexpected and uncontrollable circumstances, the result will be a life lived from the standpoint of anger, disappointment, anxiety, and lack of compassion - not to mention the biological responses that result like muscle tension and stress-related disease. The mechanism we need to employ is acceptance.

Cultivating acceptance

There is a simple truth that we must acknowledge: In our earthly plane of existence things are not perfect and never will be. There is a downside to nearly everything. Ironically, managing to frame your everyday experience to incorporate this principle will lead you to a more peaceful and complete life. Here are some tips for cultivating acceptance in your life:

- Choose happiness. Happiness is an inner choice that is independent of external circumstances.

- Focus on the wonderful. There is something awe-inspiring about almost every circumstance and occurrence. Even after the tragic events of 911, beauty arose out of the ashes as people from every race and creed bound themselves together with cords of love and compassion and labored toward a common and collective goal - helping their fellow man.

- Forego comparisons, as there will always be somebody who has a better job, a bigger house, or better hair than you. Choose to focus on, accept, and embrace what you have been given. And watch happiness ensue.

- See yourself in a new light. In one sense, you are divinely created. In another, you are but dust. We exist in a place where those two states of being are not mutually exclusive.

At some level, we all realize that life can be unpredictable and there are things that we cannot change. Yet many of our thoughts, beliefs, and actions continuously contradict this simple truth. Indeed, one of the biggest sources of unhappiness is striving to correct, modify, reverse, deny or otherwise not accept what we cannot change. In broad terms, people are equal on the playing field of life in that they are seeking some of the same things - happiness, peace, and harmony. In order to reach those ends, we must learn to cultivate the ability to embrace and accept with conscious understanding those things we cannot change.

Challenge Your Tightest-Held Beliefs

"Doubt everything. Find your own light."

~Siddhartha Gautama

*B*eliefs are complicated elements of human existence. They shape our destiny and color our world. They serve as rudders that guide our emotions and steer our actions. In essence, beliefs are simply thoughts about ourselves, the world and others that we assume to be true. A person's belief system is like a rule book that serves as a basis for governing our internal attitudes and, ultimately, our outward behavior.

Where do beliefs come from?

The formation of a belief system begins from the time that we are able to comprehend words. Beliefs are instilled into our subconscious mind by those whom we regard as authority figures such as parents, teachers, and community leaders. Some beliefs are highly beneficial in that they open up new possibilities and expand a person's positive experiences. But others serve to limit us and cage our potential. Whether positive or negative, beliefs exert a commanding influence on our capacity to experience success and happiness in life.

The power of beliefs

The supreme driving force that either inspires us or disables us is underwritten by our core beliefs. This powerful system determines our capacity to experience success in life or convinces us that we are doomed for failure. Those who possess a belief system that is built on optimism and positive principles have a greater chance for achievements in their lives even in the face of overwhelming odds.

Once a person begins to establish success in their lives, it reinforces the beliefs that they hold. Unfortunately, it works in the negative as well. For instance, if you want to learn to play the piano and you believe that you can, you will begin to pick up on musical principles and will soon be playing melodious pieces. However, if you believe that you cannot play the piano, you will look for evidence that verifies that belief – no matter how erroneous it may be. You might cite the fact that nobody in your family ever played a musical instrument. And chances are you will only hear and acknowledge the mistakes that you make sitting at the piano bench – not the correctly played compositions.

Challenging your beliefs

Identifying, confronting, challenging, and changing your limiting beliefs can be hard work, but it can be some of the most important work you will ever do. And it can yield great results. This endeavor starts by becoming aware of what you believe. To do this, begin keeping a journal of your inner dialogue. Write down every time you call yourself stupid, clumsy, or otherwise inept. Record your emotional state as well as how you feel. Emotions are the direct result of thoughts and beliefs. Over time, you will start to see a pattern from which you can analyze your core beliefs. Here are more steps to take in challenging and changing your beliefs:

- Address your fears. Belief systems are largely built upon fears. Some were justified when we were children, but don't serve us anymore in adulthood. For example, a child holds their mother's hand in a supermarket because they fear getting lost. In adulthood, however, that belief is no longer useful in most cases. If we continue to carry the same notions into adulthood, it will likely cause us to behave in irrational ways.

- Observe your speech. You may think you are fully aware of the meaning of your words, yet many times your speech actually reveals your subconscious beliefs. For example, recall how many times you comment on how depressing the weather is. The underlying premise behind that statement is that the amount of water falling from the sky has power over how happy or sad you become. And this belief is reinforced every time you make this sort of remark.

- Pay attention to what you can't do. Make a list of things that you feel you cannot do. This list will give you valuable insights into what you believe about yourself and your limitations. And it will also explain the basis for much of the action you take or don't take. For example, if you think you cannot obtain a high paying job then you will not even bother to apply for executive positions. Or, if you believe that you cannot lose weight then you probably will not stick with an exercise program long enough to see any results.

Our core beliefs significantly affect the outcomes that we experience in life. They form the foundation for the thoughts we have and the decisions we make. Beliefs serve as the mind map of the world we chose to live in. Questioning our belief system is sometimes scary, because our perception of reality is at stake. But it's only by challenging our most tightly held beliefs that we become able to change our reality in positive ways.

Learn to be Uncomfortable

"It's good to do uncomfortable things.
It's weight training for life."

~*Anne Lamott*

*U*nless you're willing to repeatedly step beyond your comfortable boundaries, you'll never know how far you can travel in your own life. Indeed, reward is almost always tied to moving out of one's comfort zone and into some sort of risk. Stay comfortable and your existence may be a safe one, but it will also be weighed down by its own inertia, deprived of challenge and flow. Learn to be comfortable being uncomfortable and you'll find plentiful opportunities to let your life energies spill over the "prescribed limits" that you'd previously believed in.

This involves saying "yes" even when the safety-seeker inside of you wants to say "no." Or, if you can't say yes then at least allow yourself a "maybe." Growth and expansion necessitate movement. When we are comfortable, we are also stationary. There are times when this has value, such as when we're in need of rest and recuperation on physical, mental and emotional levels. But such a stance can also become a person's primary response to life. A person will never know the richness and variety of experience that might have been possible had he or she always decided to play it safe.

The advantages of living outside of your comfort zone
Learn to be comfortable being uncomfortable and life can

continually surprise you. Doors open where you thought there were only walls. Surprise, after all, is one result of encountering the unknown; and to be comfortable means to stay within the bounds of the known. We are comfortable when life is familiar, but the fact that it is familiar does not necessarily make it satisfying or fulfilling.

In fact, we humans are quite adaptable and we can adjust even to miserable conditions to such an extent that unhappiness becomes our normal mode of operation. For such people "comfortable" entails some form of suffering – because this is what they have always known, and they're scared (for whatever reason) of stepping out from under that familiar umbrella.

Learn to be comfortable being uncomfortable and you may soon be wondering how your old restrictive world ever could have felt like it was big enough for you.

How do you move beyond your old boundaries?

Making this sort of risk-taking a part of your daily practice is relatively simple. Think of an area of your life where you feel limited, and then find some small way to act differently, as though that limitation was not a reality. If you're lonely, simply smiling at or saying hello to a stranger can encourage you to begin seeing yourself as not so alone after all. If you feel like a social misfit, alienated by society, you may find that taking the risk – even once a day – to speak your mind around others can work to challenge that conviction. People may surprise you, their responses contradicting your belief about yourself.

We can only step away from our old notions and into a newer and wider world if we learn to be comfortable being uncomfortable and begin thinking and acting in ways that we've never dared to before.

It's Okay to Be Imperfect

"My imperfections and failures are as much a blessing from God as my successes and my talents."

~Mahatma Gandhi

From a young age we are pressured to live up to certain standards and in many cases these standards are simply unreasonable. Your hair must be perfectly straight instead of frizzy or you are not beautiful enough. You must get straight As on your report card - even one B is a sign of failure. You must pitch a perfect no-hitter baseball game or forget your chances of getting accepted to college on a scholarship.

We hear these messages that encourage perfection from our parents, friends, significant others, teachers, coworkers, favorite television characters and even people we meet on the street. Many times these people do not understand how their words can hurt. In some cases, they are dealing with their own fruitless battle of striving for perfection.

These messages stick with us longer than we are willing to admit. Perfection-seeking children can turn into irrational, controlling adults. At some point we have to make peace with ourselves and realize that no matter how hard we try, we will always be beautifully imperfect human beings.

How to Make Peace with Imperfection
The pursuit of perfection is an addiction and, as with any

addiction, the first step is admitting to yourself that you have a problem. It is not healthy to become angry and mope around for a whole day because you didn't get a perfect score on a video game. You are not a bad citizen because you were late paying a bill one month. If you have these types of thoughts or reactions to what you perceive as "failure" you may have a problem.

Once you accept the fact that you are striving for unrealistic standards, the next step is to find the root of the problem. If you had to pick two people or influences that made you into a perfection-seeker, who would they be? Your parents? A character on a television show that you loved to watch as a youngster? Maybe you were in a bad relationship with someone who tore down your self-esteem. Did anyone make you feel as if you were not enough if you did not live up to his or her standards? Understand that the issue is not with you—it was with them.

Finally, accept the fact that being imperfect is not a bad thing - in fact it can be a very good thing. It makes you unique, fun and free. For instance, you may not have 20-20 vision, but a lot of people find that glasses make them look cuter and sometimes more intelligent. You may have grown up believing that shiny straight hair is the ideal, but soon learn wearing your hair wild, frizzy and curly better fits your unique personal style. Some people believe being short is a deficiency, but if you open your eyes to the millions of other short, happy people around you instead of focusing on the benefits of being tall, you may find you wouldn't have it any other way.

Finding Peace in Imperfection Takes Time

Making peace with imperfection takes time. You can't expect a belief system that took decades to develop to melt away in hours. True change does not come instantly - it is a slow, day-by-day, step-by-step process. So take some time identifying each of your imperfections and then accept that you have limitations. If someone around you is making you feel insufficient or impeding your growth process, stay as far away from them as possible until they learn how to show you support.

No matter how long it takes you to find peace, be happy that you've at least begun the journey of embracing your imperfectly beautiful self. Make each day count.

Deliberately Become Self-Aware

"Find out who you are and do it on purpose."

~Dolly Parton

Deliberately becoming self-aware is an essential part of experiencing deeper levels of success, personal growth, and happiness. It is a delightful and fulfilling journey inward to a revealing land of self-discovery. By becoming self-aware, you will begin to understand the many facets of your nature that contribute to the way you think and behave. Whether you are looking to enrich your life, experience more happiness, or simply know yourself better, self-awareness is the pathway to understanding how you go about interacting with your surroundings.

What is self-awareness?
Since the dawn of humankind, we have benefited from living in a safe, social environment. Prehistoric people did not have choices about their roles in society. Men hunted, women tended to the domestic duties, and the children helped out whether they wanted to or not. However, as civilization advanced, our groups became more highly developed and complex. And with our sophisticated society came the advent of choice. Today, we have many options. We choose what we say, where we go, how we react, and how we will to decide to interpret the actions of others. Because of this aptitude for superior intellect and higher order thinking, it's easy for the lines of communication to become blurred in a network of thoughts and feelings. It can become harder to communicate with other people, and more importantly, it becomes difficult to understand ourselves.

In a society like ours, self-awareness is critical. If we cannot examine and understand our own imagining and motivations, how can we reach our goals?

In the simplest terms, self-awareness is the act of observing your thoughts and emotions and understanding how and why you interact with your environment and with other people. Self-awareness is an important and practical personal empowerment tool. Here are some of the aspects of yourself you will discover as you become self-aware:

- Your fears

- Your needs

- Your beliefs

- Your reactions

- Your baggage from the past

- Your dreams for the future

Becoming self-aware
If you are a person contemplating becoming self-aware, you probably have a deep curiosity into the inner workings of your own mind. But it's important to note that this exercise is not for the faint of heart. To really come to know yourself, you must ask tough questions and be willing to answer honestly. Start by directing your attention inward and allow space for self-awareness to grow by asking these questions:

- What emotions am I experiencing? Emotions are the result of thoughts and beliefs. By tracing your emotions backward, you can find a cause and effect relationship between your thoughts and feelings.
- Why am I thinking these thoughts? Analyze your thoughts and write them down. You will soon see a pattern. You

can then consciously determine whether your thought pattern is beneficial or if it needs to be changed.

- What is my intention in this circumstance? Determining the intended outcome in any given situation can give you great insight into why you behave the way you do.

- How do I talk to myself? Believe it or not, we all talk to ourselves. By sitting alone in silence you can observe the manner in which you talk to yourself and the effect it has on you. Notice if you become restless or not. Notice if you are uncomfortable. Are you at peace or in a state of turmoil? Trace these feelings back to the contents of the dialogue that caused them and take note. This will help you consciously transform negative self-talk into a more loving and supportive conversation.

- Do I feel powerless? Answering this question will reveal your deep-seated fears that need to be addressed. It will also give you clues about your individual needs and what you expect from others.

As with any skill, becoming self-aware takes perseverance and practice. The answers to the above questions may not be clear at first, but don't give up. Keep asking the questions and the answers will become more insightful as time goes on.

Self-awareness is an essential personal development skill that can be consciously expanded to enable people to become proficient at noticing how their inner and outer worlds interact. By becoming deliberately self-aware, you will soon find you are better able to navigate the challenges that come your way. Ultimately, increasing self-awareness can lead to a happier, more satisfying, and more successful life.

Chapter 2

Change What Needs Changing

"It's never too late to be what you might have been."
~George Eliot

Stop Labeling Yourself

"What labels me, negates me."
~Friedrich Nietzsche

*H*ave you ever seen somebody hold their fingers up against their forehead in the shape of an "L" indicating that somebody was a "loser?" This is not merely a description; it's what social scientists call a "label." There are many labels that people use on themselves and others. Conservative, perfectionist, religious, big-mouth and pessimist are examples of some other commonly used terms that label individuals or groups.

Why do we label?

As intelligent human beings, we seek ways to categorize the information our senses perceive. Since some of this information is complex, we look for ways to simplify it by sorting it, putting it into intellectual folders, and labeling it. It sounds like an efficient way to conduct our cognitive business, but there is a down side to this practice.

Labeling is protective and helpful in many situations. For example, many people label snakes and spiders as "dangerous." This keeps them from getting bitten. Or at the sight of a glowing red object, you may label it in your mind as "hot" and refrain from touching it. But when we start labeling ourselves or other people, the results can be destructive. Even if the label does not carry negative connotations – such as a "history major" or "housewife" – labels still leave out more information than they contain.

What happens when people get labeled?

To illustrate what happens when a label is placed on a person, I will use an example from the mental health field.

Psychiatrists feel the need to label patients with a diagnosis in order to help them. But what happens many times is the person who is labeled with a specific disorder or disease is automatically disempowered because of the label put on them. In essence, their disorder enables them to opt out of assuming responsibility for themselves. For example, when somebody is labeled with "depression" they oftentimes believe they can't help lying in bed all day, and this behavior is normal for this illness.

The same thing happens when somebody is labeled as "crazy" or we call ourselves "obsessive." Our tendency is to live up to the labels we carry.

Labels form the basis for beliefs

Labels are the short-hand or headings for a whole list of beliefs that form as a result of the interpretation of the meaning of that label. For example, if you label yourself as "fat" you tell yourself that fat people can't go out in bathing suits; they can't eat pizza; and they need to exercise a lot. These labels and the rules assigned to them become our reality and the governing beliefs by which we live. Worse yet, we come to identify with the traits dictated by the labels and we have a hard time making positive changes in our lives because the labels have become who we are. For instance, if you are not the "hot" girl in the corner office, who are you? If you are not "Edward's wife," who are you? If we let go of our labels, we fear losing our very identity.

How to peel the labels off

No doubt you have been living – probably subconsciously –

under the powerful influence of some destructive self-assigned labels. But now it's time to start consciously peeling them off.

- Start by asking yourself a simple question: Who are you? The answer to this question will give you some insight into the labels that you put on yourself. Maybe your answer would be that you are somebody's daughter, a business owner, or the kid who dropped out of high school. Whatever your answers are, write them down.

- Now contemplate where these labels may have come from. Did they come from your parents? Did they come from your own experience? Did you come up with that label?

- Ask yourself if you are living your life genuinely, or are your behavior patterns fulfilling label requirements?

- Start doing things differently. If you are a "geek," try putting on some trendy clothes. You will soon see that you have many choices as to how to think, act and be. Most importantly, you will come to realize that you are not your label.

Political and religious labels can also be limiting. On one hand it's good to have a belief system based on beneficial values. On the other, it can stop us from getting to the heart of matters. In politics, we can become so identified with the group that the ideology becomes the driving force and not the quest for solutions. In much the same way, when we label ourselves with a particular brand of religion we become closed to other perspectives, thus narrowing our exposure to new possibilities.

Labeling is a natural tendency we all have as a way of organizing information. It is a means by which we make assumptions about people by pigeonholing them into categories. In some situations, labeling is helpful. But in general, the labeling of people is not.

And it is especially harmful to label yourself. The fact is that people are too complex and unique to fall under general identifiers. In fact, the only label we can all correctly fall under is "human." One of the most liberating things we can do in the way of personal development is to discover what labels have been limiting us and confront how they have impacted our person. Then peel them away and start living a label-free life.

Stop Playing the Shame Game

"Whatever is begun in anger, ends in shame."
~Benjamin Franklin

A person's self-image has a strong influence over the life experiences that he or she will encounter. We all have some fairly concrete internal images about ourselves, and they act like magnets, drawing experiences into our life that mirror who we think we are. Among other things, these images tell us how much we are supposedly worth. And many of the messages we receive are unfortunately driven by an underlying sense of shame.

We need to stop playing the shame game
There's a plethora of books and articles offering advice to help people to improve their self-image and, as a result, live a life free from shame. This literature provides guidance to a person who struggles with shame issues, although much of it does not address the many factors that contribute to a person's sense of shame. Self-image is composed not only of our ideas about ourselves, but also our ideas about ourselves in relation to the world. Such ideas may revolve around any of the following themes:

- Our beliefs about age, aging, and our own place in the scheme of time.

- Our racial heritage and our underlying feelings about it.

- Our body-image as well as any cultural notions we may

have accepted regarding the definition of the "ideal body type."

- Our gender and our beliefs about the nature and value of that gender.

- Our occupation and any attitudes we may have taken on regarding the worth of our work.

- Our ability to relate to others on mental and emotional levels.

This is a partial list. As you can see, personal convictions may have to be examined if we want to know why we don't feel worthy of a lucrative job, a loving mate, or good health.

Is there any justification for shame?

Shame runs deep in many men and women, and it serves no constructive purpose. It doesn't teach us how to find happiness, how to expand our lives or how to better ourselves. Shame basically accomplishes two things: (1) It keeps us from treating ourselves with patience and compassion, and (2) it keeps us from using our gifts and abilities in the world where they might benefit others. Everyone loses.

We stop playing the shame game by forgiving ourselves and gifting ourselves with regular doses of self-love. This may involve owning up to the pain that we have been carrying inside ourselves. It may mean admitting that we feel fear. Shame is a blanket. It's not a feeling, per se, but rather a layer of self-recrimination that smothers other feelings. Under its influence, we don't feel worthy of anything, even our own sensations of hurt and joy. Shame is a numbing agent, which separates us from ourselves and from others.

Learn to identify the beliefs you hold on to that feed into your false sense of shame. They are the personal convictions that are uniquely yours. Once we know what those false beliefs are, and we have dragged them into the light of day, we can discard them. We can stop playing the shame game and start playing the game of living and learning. We can fall down and pick ourselves back up again without judgment.

Stop Blaming Yourself and Others

"When you blame others,
you give up your power to change."

~Robert Anthony

Of all the games that we humans play, the blame game is one of the most ineffective and destructive. It has been the underlying cause of a considerable amount of damage ranging from hostility between nations to conflicts between husbands and wives. And we harm ourselves by playing it alone, as well.

How we play the blame game
In essence, the blame game begins when we are confronted with an undesirable situation. The object is to determine who caused the situation and persist in keeping the focus on that person instead of taking steps to repair the situation. The best players have irrational beliefs that help them compete like professionals. They believe the cause of a situation is external and must be identified. Oftentimes, they feel the perpetrator must be punished in some way for their misconduct. Ask yourself these questions:

- Have you ever blamed traffic for your late arrival?

- Have you ever blamed your busy schedule for your inability to exercise?

- Have you ever blamed your kids for your bad day?

25

Players of the blame game also have a hard time separating the action from the person. Consequently, the person who "did it" deserves to be looked down upon, ostracized, stigmatized, alienated or otherwise disrespected.

Taking personal responsibility

There are many people who have gotten very good at playing the blame game, but these people are generally not good at taking personal responsibility. When the blame is constantly shifted to others, it is a clear indication the blamer perceives themselves as a victim. They feel external circumstances are the reason for all their hardships and they feel helpless to affect change in their lives. Taking personal responsibility is the first step towards freedom from the victim mentality. Here are a few signs that you may not be taking personal responsibility:

- You believe you are never wrong.

- You use other people's negligent behavior to justify your own.

- You don't feel that you can do anything to make your life change for the better.

- You often feel sorry for yourself.

Taking responsibility versus blaming yourself

As a part of life, bad things do happen. Many of these things we cannot control. We don't control the type of parents we have, where we were born or our genetic disposition. Because of this, it's important to understand taking personal responsibility for our attitudes, thoughts, and behavior is not the same as taking the blame for things outside of our control. On the contrary, taking responsibility is more about empowering yourself by taking control of our reaction to difficulties. Here are some signs that you may be engaging in self-blame:

- When something bad happens, do you wonder what you did to deserve it?

- Do you think that you always have "bad luck"?

- Do you often think that you should have done things differently?

This kind of thinking is highly counterproductive because it spotlights what you did and how things went wrong instead of focusing on healthy attitudes and solutions to the problem.

How to opt out of the blame game

Life is funny in that it will keep throwing you the same ball until you catch it. The same lessons keep being handed back to us until we learn them. Here are some things to consider the next time you are tempted to blame yourself or others for your ill fate:

- Don't expect perfection. Whether we are talking about you or somebody else, the fact of the matter is that we are all flawed. Mistakes will happen and finding somebody to blame never fixes the situation.

- Adopt the belief that there is something to be learned from your circumstance. You must be willing to learn lessons in life in order to grow.

- Accept yourself. Ironically, having a loving and accepting attitude toward yourself will help you have the same attitude towards others.

Most games are fun, but the blame game will leave you in a bad place, often feeling like a victim. And what good does finding somebody to blame do anyway? The mistake has happened. No amount of blame is going to correct the situation. One of the biggest personal development steps you can take is to stop reactively playing the blame game. Start proactively taking responsibility for your own life and happiness.

Give up Something You Don't Need

"We must be willing to let go of the life we planned so as to have the life that is waiting for us."

~Joseph Campbell

There are incidents in our daily world that constrict the flow of life, bringing it to a halt at times. For example, a collision on the highway may back up traffic for miles. It's easy to see how such a circumstance can quite literally block one's movement and freedom.

It is oftentimes not as easy to see how our personal lives and our internal environments can become similarly clogged, denying us opportunities for growth and flow. Oftentimes these barriers are created for us because we are clinging to certain beliefs, habits or personal relationships that we no longer need. In such situations, we are giving our energy over to something that gives us little or no return. When you give up something you don't need, then you release that energy from its place of being stuck. It is then yours to use and to put to more creative, life-expanding purposes.

The first step in giving up something you don't need is to locate the "clogs" in your life. Where are your emotional, financial and spiritual resources being dammed up? Is it in an addiction of some kind? Or is it in situations involving needy friends who never return the favor? What about emotional dramas revolving around other people that don't need to be your concern? Once you've identified an area where you're being drained you can stop focusing your attention on the situation and effectively plug up the hole.

Everything that we claim ownership of in our lives becomes invested with our psychic energy. This is true even of seemingly trivial things like an unflattering outfit that you never wear but still keep in the dresser. Why not get rid of it, and free yourself of something that fails to uphold your self-image in a positive way?

What's the payoff for giving things up?

Sometimes, in order to move in a positive direction, we have to first relinquish the dead weight in our lives that's dragging us down. This may involve taking personal inventory and examining aspects of our experience that were previously taken for granted. We may come up against some of our blind spots and realize that certain things that we thought were essential to our well-being are decidedly not. There will be questions - perhaps uncomfortable questions - that rise up and need answering. Here are a few possible examples:

- Does this person really care for me, or is he or she mainly interested in drawing my energy and attention?

- Do I wear these clothes, read these books, or listen to this music anymore?

- Is it necessary for me to take on the crises of my family members, friends, and coworkers?

- Can I give up some measure of control over my children's lives and trust them to make good choices on their own?

Whenever you realize that you have invested your energy or resources into a person, place or behavior, and very little is being returned on the investment you have made, take steps to let that particular liability go. Give up something you don't need and you'll create more space for the things that are important in your life.

Practice Not Being Angry

"Angry people are not always wise."

~Jane Austen

*D*o you believe there are certain events or behaviors that make you angry? In all truthfulness, there aren't. Nothing can "make" you angry; you decide whether you will get angry or not. While there may be triggers that create situations in which you are prone to get angry, ultimately it comes down to a decision that you and you alone make.

Imagine you are at home in the midst of a heated argument when suddenly the phone rings. How do you answer it? Do you answer with levels of vengeance detectable in your voice? No, it is more likely that you answer courteously. You intentionally set your anger aside long enough to take the call.

As another example, picture yourself driving in the car with your family. You're on a tight schedule and your children's dawdling has caused you to be late for an important event. You may be fuming at them as you drive en route, but once you arrive at your destination, you take on a different persona. You choose not to be angry anymore so you can interact sociably with others at the event.

In both these cases, you intentionally made the decision not to be angry. While you might have the impression that your anger is dependent solely on your feelings—particularly your feelings of hurt, fear, or frustration—the truth is that you have a choice in the matter.

If you have a history of giving in to every opportunity to become angry, it will not be an easy transition to decide not to be angry. Your goal may be to become angry less easily, but you will likely still find yourself losing control from time to time. This will continue until you develop some self-discipline. Unfortunately, self-discipline does not develop overnight. Through the practice of resisting becoming angry, though, you will gradually develop that discipline.

An old Hebrew proverb states, *"Fools vent their anger, but the wise quietly hold it back."*

Will you resolve to temper your anger, or will you foolishly continue to vent it, making yourself look foolish in the process?

The choice is yours.

Don't be Afraid to Ask for Help

*"And, when you want something, all the universe conspires in
helping you to achieve it."*

~Paulo Coelho

*F*or the first couple of centuries of its existence, the United
States was largely built upon the ethics of self-sufficiency. It
was called rugged individualism back in the days when America
still had a wild frontier that "needed conquering." This is a life
philosophy many of us in the West have inherited to some extent
or another. Many people still hear that voice inside of them saying
they should be a Jack or Jill of all trades and asking for help is a
sign of weakness.

The "go it alone" philosophy has set its roots deep within the psyche
of modern man. Such thinking has influenced our major religions
and sciences and encouraged us to see ourselves as separate
from the rest of nature. This philosophy led to the Industrial
Revolution and later, the computer age. In recent decades it has
begun showing its darker face more in the form of ecological
devastation, depletion of resources, and overpopulation.

The great challenge of our age is to once again see ourselves
as an integral part of the whole web of life. We need the spirit
of cooperation much more than we need rugged individualism
nowadays. The truth is that nothing and no one is completely
self-sufficient. All of life depends upon other life.

It's natural to ask for help when you're in need

When it comes to cooperation, society imitates nature. In the natural world, the various species of life have unique adaptations and abilities. Together they form a balanced ecosystem that supplies each group with what it needs to survive. In the social world, people have unique talents as well as different areas of lack. There may be plumbers out there who write inspired verse in their spare time, but we don't typically expect a plumber to be a great poet. What's more, if we all knew how to fix pipes then plumbers would all be out of work. Asking for help in the social world means not only acknowledging your limitations but also giving others the opportunity to put their special talents to use.

Don't be afraid to ask for help

Reaching out teaches us humility. We can learn a lot about the graceful "give and take" that exists at the heart of good human relationships. Whether your struggles are material, emotional, or spiritual in nature, chances are someone out there understands the battle you're waging better than you do. And they may be grateful for the chance to help you.

Asking for help can go a long way towards opening up channels of communication and bringing people closer together. For example, when you reach out to friends they have the opportunity to show you empathy even if they can't solve your problem. Asking for help is an act of vulnerability. When we are exposed in this way our masks come off and people are able to see our more authentic self. And we also see them on a deeper level as well. We admit our humanness and, by extension, give others permission to be human as well. The moments in life when you might seize the opportunity to reach out rather than "tough it all out alone" include:

- When you're feeling bereaved after losing a loved one or find yourself in the wake of a failed relationship.

- When it's your first day in a new school, or you're at a party or other gathering where you don't know anyone.

- When you are having health concerns and you need some physical or emotional support.

Being vulnerable and asking for help in those kinds of situations creates an opening through which support, empathy, and cooperation can enter our lives. We may form new friendships as a result. In addition, we might learn new information, skills, life approaches, and philosophies.

Most of all, we may come away from the experience feeling like we're not so alone in the world after all.

Chapter 3

Engage in Constant Learning

*"Live as if you were to die tomorrow.
Learn as if you were to live forever."*

~Mahatma Gandhi

Cultivate Curiosity
(Ask "What" Instead of "Why")

*"Sometimes the questions are complicated
and the answers are simple."*

~Dr. Seuss

*I*t's safe to say that we live in a culture that discourages curiosity. Based upon assembly-line modes of action and thought, so much of our society's daily life is geared towards expedience. Because of this, it is much more profitable to "know" than it is to "wonder." We receive this message quite frequently and in many forms from a very young age. It gradually assumes a stronger hold on our psyches as time goes on and none of us escape its influence completely.

Why should you cultivate curiosity?
Those of us who want to cultivate curiosity would do well to observe young children and the ways in which they think and behave. This is the true magic of childhood - we possess fresh minds when we are young. We haven't yet become concerned with the uses of things. Rather, we're more interested in what things actually are– their states of being. For example, a child would be more likely think, "What is that furry little creature running around there?" Whereas, an adult will more likely inquire, "Why is that groundhog in my garden?"

Curiosity is worth being cultivated because it brings us in touch with the vital feeling of being alive and also awakens a sense of adventure. Curiosity seeks the "what" of existence. What can my body do? What is this feeling? What is possible for me today? Without curiosity we are left with the status quo. We are left with a life that has been explained – perhaps by science, religion, political rhetoric, or job training – and has been stripped of its evocative magic.

Frequently we only want to know why, and why is oftentimes concerned with the relation of things to the status quo. Why do those people look different? Why is he walking like that? Why does she always wear those colors? If the status quo is accepted as the only worthwhile reality, then there will be an underlying sense that individuals should somehow justify why they are the way they are and why they act the way they do. The curious mind, on the other hand, doesn't need justifications because it is ruled by a singular passion - to explore the possibilities of the moment.

How can you honor curiosity in your daily life?
Cultivating curiosity requires of us a certain amount of courage and resolve. The forces of fear at work within society (and within us) urge us to keep our world small and contained. Mind your own business. Stick close to your own kind. Follow proper procedures. If in doubt, ask someone in a position of authority. Cultivating curiosity means stepping away from the assembly-line mentality and simply asking: What else is out there, and what else is within me?

This can involve a whole shift in perspective that has to do with the ways in which we see ourselves and our world. But we can take small strides along this path on a daily basis. Some of these steps can include:

- Striking up a conversation with someone whom you've seen before but never spoken to

- Taking a different route home from work.

- Visiting a new website or blog

- Trying new foods

- Experimenting with different styles of dress

You're cultivating your curiosity with any of these approaches if the more cautious part of your mind begins to get a little frightened. The assembly-line mind would rather judge than explore. It likes to feel as though the territory has already all been mapped out. But magical mind – the childlike mind – is ruled by curiosity, knowing that there are always new landscapes and wonders around the bend.

Step Out of Your Comfort Zone

"Do one thing every day that scares you."

~Eleanor Roosevelt

*R*emaining trapped in your comfort zone can cause you to lose many opportunities, miss out on exhilarating experiences, and feel confined in a mediocre life. For these reasons, it's important that you learn how to step out of your self-imposed boundaries in order to enjoy life. The first step to accomplishing this is to have the desire to change. The next step is to take action. Here are some ways to allow yourself to enjoy life by leaving your comfort zone.

Make a fool out of yourself

More than likely you feel resistant to this concept because you are worried about what other people will think of you. This fear regarding the opinions of others often holds us back from taking risks. By overcoming this fear, you can be yourself and avoid allowing anxiety to have such a tight grasp on your life. Take a deep, soothing breath and then do something silly in public. Have a good laugh about it with a friend. At the end of the day, you will have a new exciting memory stored in your mind and feel more open and relaxed. One day, you will wake up and realize it doesn't matter what others think about you.

Hang out with someone who is willing to be crazy

Another great way to step out of your comfort zone is to hang out with someone who is crazy, since that helps bring out your

41

wild side. The people you are friends with tend to influence you, whether in a miniscule, moderate, or huge way. There is a strong possibility you find out how much fun you can have while hanging out with someone who is adventurous and spontaneous. If you want to step out of your comfort zone, you may as well have fun doing so. Isn't that the point, after all?

Overcome a fear

What better way to step out of your comfort zone than to overcome a fear? To conquer a fear, you must force yourself to do something that frightens you. Don't spend too much time deciding which fear you want to overcome or you will procrastinate. If you are struggling with choosing, then have someone else decide for you or close your eyes and pick something randomly.

Making a fool out of yourself, hanging out with someone who is crazy, and overcoming a fear are powerful techniques for stepping out of your comfort zone. At first, it may be difficult to implement these concepts, but it will be worth it in the end. You can kiss your ordinary life good bye and welcome more exciting, thrilling, and fulfilling adventures.

Get Out of Your Rut

"Life is like riding a bicycle.
To keep your balance, you must keep moving."

~Albert Einstein

*W*e are creatures of habit and so we tend to do the same things day in and day out. Yes, life is busy and this may be why so many people fall into these ruts. We believe we can't squeeze any more time into our day in order to do something fun or unusual.

A person with a demanding career, or the parent with a family and home to manage, might find that circumstances dictate how they use the best hours of their time. Before they know it, they have little "me" time left and any fun times seem to be over. Change might be what these people are needing, although it seems to be too much work to make it happen. The truth is that life can become richer when things are mixed up a little.

Break out of your mold
If you are ready to block out some time to work on your own "project happiness," you can start by making a decision regarding when and how you will make the needed changes. Will you pursue a one-time event? Will you plan to do something daily at a specific time? Will you embark on your plan alone or with someone else?

Taking on and accomplishing challenges opens the way for greater fulfillment. And remember that a challenge is more than merely a goal. The word "challenge" implies something that needs an act of bravery, persistence, or pushing oneself in some way. This may involve choosing something a little out of character for yourself.

Take steps

Taking steps to challenge yourself will help change your paradigm. As you make a new plan you will begin to see the world differently. You will see yourself rising above the mundane as you begin a path of discovery. You might even feel young again.

For your first challenge, you might choose something as small as trying a new restaurant or as complicated as creating art that you will try to sell. You might choose running a half-marathon or growing a great pumpkin for a fall fair. Once you choose your challenge, plan the steps you're going to take to get there.

For a quick upturn in your mood, try to challenge yourself with something you can do immediately. Throw caution to the wind by going hiking after work instead of home to cook dinner. Drive home a different way and stop at a unique deli or farmers market to purchase fresh foods. Challenging yourself to do something away from home is helpful in refreshing the spirit because you're seeing what's going on beyond your own four walls.

Get started

Are you ready to start your challenge? If so, then get out there and buy those concert tickets or the canvases and paints you'll need to start your artwork. Try a new coffee. Collect pretty rocks along a water's edge. Gather wild flowers and press them.

Enjoy the change

Your challenge isn't meant to become one more thing on your to-do list. There should be fun involved, and it should include enough variety to wake up your spirit in some way. Take in the colors, sounds, and aromas while fulfilling your challenge. Notice the beauty all around you. People watch. Laugh. Sing. Take photos. Start a conversation with a stranger.

Enjoy the reward

Challenges require a person create short-term goals that involve both discipline and action. As a result, challenges can be invigorating and motivating. Completing a challenge offers a person a sense of satisfaction and provides something to talk about with others and opens the door to interesting conversations.

Don't spend one more day resenting your life. Start with a simple challenge and then add another. There is no one else that's going to shake up your life for you, so get out there and experience life on your terms!

Learn From Your Mistakes

"Anyone who had never made a mistake
has never tried anything new."

~*Albert Einstein*

Mistakes – everyone makes them from time to time. Indeed, making a mistake can be viewed as a common experience among humankind. The only people who have never made a mistake are the ones who have never lived.

There is nothing special or unique about missteps in judgments, actions or thinking. What is special, however, is learning from that mistake. Failure to learn means you are likely to repeat it. To turn your mistakes around and bring out the best possible outcome, here are seven helpful steps:

1. Admit you have made a mistake. Do not fall prey to the tendency to blame others, deny culpability, or rationalize the mistake away. Instead, take responsibility for yourself. Acknowledge the choices and/or actions that led to the error.

2. Identify the cause of the mistake. For example, attempting to use your debit card to pay for lunch when you have insufficient funds to do so is a mistake with several potential causes. Figure out the exact nature of the mistake so you can address it head on, and avoid it happening again.

3. Do what you can to rectify the problem. If your mistake has harmed another, make amends to the best of your ability. Extend an apology, ask for forgiveness, and atone for the damage.

4. Learn what you can, then move on. A mistake is not the end of the story. Life goes on. As Thomas Edison is often credited as saying in reference to his unsuccessful experiments, "I have not failed. I've just found 10,000 ways that won't work."

5. Recognize some mistakes are inevitable. Sometimes things just happen. Stubbing your toe on the bathroom door, for example, is not something you plan to do, nor is it the result of the choices you make – at least not the conscious ones. There will be times when you are distracted and you simply make a mistake. Relax. It's not the end of the world.

6. Make the necessary adjustments to avoid the same mistake again. You do not fail when you make a mistake. You fail when you refuse to learn from your mistake. Every mistake you make is a life lesson that can be turned around to your benefit. For that to become reality, however, you must be ready and willing to apply the lessons learned.

7. Place yourself in situations where you can make even more mistakes. Not the same mistakes, mind you, but different mistakes. The only way to avoid mistakes completely is by never attempting anything. Like the turtle, you will never make progress or accomplish anything of significance unless you're willing to stick your neck out.

Many people see mistakes as a reason for shame and embarrassment. However, the truth is that making mistakes is an unavoidable part of life. They open up opportunities to learn and to grow. Do not allow your mistakes to become failures. Rather, transform your mistakes into the foundation for future success.

Fail at Something

"Success is not final, failure is not fatal:
it is the courage to continue that counts."

~*Winston S. Churchill*

*T*here are many things that can bog us down on our path and slow us down or even halt our progress, making us feel stuck at a certain bend in the road. One of the strongest forces that can hold us back is the fear of making mistakes. This fear basically says, "Until I know for certain that I'll succeed, I don't even want to try." Think about what a wider array of experiences we could open ourselves up to if we gave ourselves permission to fail at something.

Give yourself permission to be imperfect
The human experience is essentially about learning. The concept of perfection has generated a lot of stress and suffering for many people. And if any of us were actually living out the implications of this notion then we probably wouldn't be in this world to begin with. We learn as toddlers do - stumbling, falling, and picking ourselves up again. The prospect of actually walking across the room and pushing past our perceived limitations is enough to inspire us to keep trying. A child who was overly concerned with getting it right the first time would never rise up off the floor.

Be prepared and willing to fail at something and you will discover aspects of your own talents and resources that you never suspected before. You may even succeed and thereby broaden your whole self-image. But even if you don't, you will at least enjoy the learning process a lot more than you would have if you are laden with detrimental ideals of perfection.

Grant yourself the space to try and fail

Some people wish for their own private slope to practice on so they can become expert skiers before they go and do it in front of onlookers. Some only confess romantic feelings to another if they're fairly certain those feelings will be reciprocated. Some sing in the shower but never on stage at an open microphone. For such people, certain dreamed-of experiences may never move beyond the realm of fantasy. By insisting on perfection, your life will be restricted to the narrow band of activities that you can perform with ease or by look good doing. Giving yourself permission to fail at something will significantly broaden your field of possibilities.

Give some of these things a try (however clumsily):

- Dancing. The need to "get it right" can rob you of a lot of joy and expression.

- Music. How many people never pick up an instrument because they believe they're "not musical?"

- Art. Concerns about form, proportion and realism never deter a child from enjoying this activity, so why should they deter you?

- Skiing or ice skating. So what if you fall down a lot!

- Visits to the gym. Who cares what "the beautiful" people think about your body?

- Submitting prose, poetry, and artwork to various publications. You might me surprised at the outcome.

You may not even realize how many possibilities in your life you have let pass by simply because you felt like you couldn't succeed. Give yourself permission to fail and live your life more fully.

Chapter 4

Make A Daily Connection

"The simple things are also the most extraordinary things,
and only the wise can see them."

~Paulo Coelho

Commit an Act of Compassion Each Day

"Be kind, for everyone you meet
is fighting a harder battle."

~Plato

Our world is starved for love. There is a vacuum that is left behind in love's absence. Many people are trying to fill the emptiness by taking a self-destructive road to numbness – alcoholism, drug use, work addiction, promiscuity and other compulsive behaviors. In the face of suffering of such magnitude, many individuals feel compelled to embark upon personal crusades to put an end to the pain in the world. In reality we cannot end all suffering. What we can do is be a source of light to others, without martyring ourselves or attempting grand gestures that are beyond our strength and resources.

If you commit only one act of compassion each day, then you can rest assured your presence in the world becomes a beacon of hope for others. And these need not be grandiose acts.

How do you express compassion?
Compassion requires us to first recognize another's suffering. We can offer neither help nor empathy to someone else if we don't perceive their needs. Therefore, if you intend to commit an act of compassion each day, the first thing you must do is extend your awareness beyond your own concerns, worries, and hurts. Allow your perceptions to extend out from your own comfortable boundaries to encompass those around you.

This first act allows you to understand the pain and suffering of others. The next step is to realize for every need there is a remedy. Oftentimes, people do not help others because they are so thoroughly convinced that this is a world of scarcity. A scarcity mentality tells us there isn't enough to go around, so we'd better hold on to every advantage and give nothing away. Love, on the other hand, tells us that everyone benefits when we give.

Express your compassion every day
When we take on a world view of lack and scarcity, everyone must fight for their own piece of turf because another's gain will be their loss. This is an illusion. By expressing compassion we can sustain each other. Compassion involves an understanding that each person has unique gifts and things of value to offer the world. Therefore you don't need to be wealthy to be generous and compassionate. You don't need piles of money to do any of the following:

- Hold the door for an elderly or handicapped person.

- Write to a friend whom you haven't talked to in a long time.

- Say hello to someone who appears lonely.

- Take the time to listen when someone close to you wants to unload their troubles, worries or hurts.

Committing an act of compassion each day requires us to be open to and accepting of our own feelings. If we are carrying around some pain that we don't want to acknowledge or feel, then we are likely to close down when confronted by another's need, for fear that this will touch upon our own pain. The next time you feel yourself wanting to retreat when someone is opening up to you about their sorrows and struggles, ask yourself what feelings of your own are being triggered. Acknowledging our own hurt and suffering puts us in closer connection with the pain of others, but the cycle doesn't end there. Ultimately healing our own pain leads us back to love – that all-powerful force that expresses itself in the world through acts of compassion.

Connect with a Stranger

"A friend may be waiting behind a stranger's face."

~Maya Angelou

Socially speaking, our society strongly encourages us to stay within our respective niches. We tend to interact with our core group of friends and associates while the rest of humanity largely slips under our radar. Work schedules have a lot to do with this tendency. We continue to pack more working hours into a week than we once did. This means that most of us spend a good portion of our waking hours in the workplace, and we also tend to become exclusively acquainted with our co-workers due to the amount of time we spend with them. On the other hand, alternatives to the typical 9-to-5 job, such as various work-at-home scenarios, encourage us to isolate. In either case, we're leading lifestyles in which the vast majority of people in our surrounding communities remain strangers.

The need to connect with strangers

Being out of touch with the people in our communities is not beneficial to our mental, emotional, and spiritual well-being. We need to interact with people from walks of life that are different from our own. Exposing ourselves to different perspectives, attitudes and knowledge enriches and expands our lives. Even knowing this, we may still struggle with the question of how to connect with strangers while we're locked into our relatively closed social environments.

How do you enter into another person's orbit?

Reaching out to strangers requires a measure of courage and initiative. We have to risk being vulnerable. When you approach a stranger you open yourself up to the possibility of meeting with virtually any kind of reaction. You may be rejected, shunned, or even find yourself on the receiving end of some hostility. Fortunately, one reality of human nature is working in your favor: When you risk being vulnerable and act naturally, people are much more likely to lower their defenses and also be real with you. There is an opening through which real connection can occur.

Such opportunities to connect can be found in a myriad of places: the supermarket, the line at a bank or post office or any event involving the kids (if you're a parent). The people you approach may be longing for connection as much as you are. They could be secretly relieved and grateful you approached and gave them an opening.

Strangers broaden our social worlds

If you make the effort to connect with a stranger every day your whole world can broaden dramatically. Opportunities present themselves to do things you've never done, think thoughts that never occurred to you before and see life in new and different ways. Social interaction is much broader and richer than many of us realize simply because we so often move within familiar orbits. Breaking such habits does require some effort, and it can also require facing some fear. But the outcome of taking the risk can totally transform our image of ourselves and others. This plays out in obvious and dramatic ways during times of crisis such as in the course of a natural disaster. People come together like never before. They pitch in to help each other survive and recover even if they have scarcely spoken before the disaster hit. Lonely and isolated men and women find it within themselves to reach out for help or to lend others a hand.

Here are a few approaches to consider:

- Smiling at someone you pass as you're walking, rather than turning your eyes down towards the sidewalk.

- Actually saying hello instead of just smiling or nodding.

- Introducing yourself to someone who you may have seen around but have never spoken to before.

- In any social situation, voicing aloud some thought or funny observation you may have instead of keeping it to yourself - even when you're surrounded by people who you don't know.

The occasions upon which you reach out and connect with strangers don't need to be that dramatic. Adjusting some of your habits so that they become more welcoming rather than guarded can go a long way towards fostering new connections.

Listen More Than You Talk

"Courage is what it takes to stand up and speak;
courage is also what it takes to sit down and listen."

~*Winston S. Churchill*

*M*y father would frequently say "God gave us two ears and one mouth, so that we can listen more than we talk." And Judge Judy is font of admonishing those in front of her "to remember to put on their listening ears."

Authentic listening is an important skill that can help each of us become a better parent, a better friend, a better mate, a better manager and a better employee. We can reap those benefits by simply improving the way we approach the concept of listening.

The majority of us have adequate hearing capabilities, yet we don't use our ears to listen. We may think we are listening, but most of the time when someone is talking to us, we are mentally somewhere else. Listening effectively involves more than simply sitting passively in a room while someone else talks.

Two-way communication
Communication is a two-way street. There is a person who is attempting to send a message and there is a person who is trying to receive a message. For communication to be effective, the listener must hear the same message the speaker was sending.

Sometimes the reason there is a miscommunication is because

the person who is doing the talking is not very effective. They may not know how to successfully get their message across.

At other times, the fault may lie with the listener who is not paying attention. He may think he already understands the message being delivered so he does not bother to listen. Or, the listener may not understand the message at all but does not want the speaker to know he doesn't understand it. And lastly, the listener may simply tune out the words to think about something else.

The best way to hear a message is to commit yourself to listening and follow these tips:

- Eliminate your mental distractions.

- Focus on the speaker and the message.

- Listen without any pre-conceived ideas.

- Listen with an open mind and an open heart.

- Don't interrupt.

- Don't argue.

If you are confused about any part of the discussion, ask the speaker to clarify the issue for you. Do not assume you have understood the message correctly without checking. If need be, tell the speaker how you interpreted their message and ask if you have understood them correctly.

These listening techniques are simple once you understand what is necessary, although it may take practice before they become second nature to you. They require being open to the message the other person is sending and sometimes it requires you to hear the implied message that underlies the message being verbalized. It requires you to recheck yourself to make sure you are hearing the message the other person is trying to send you and not simply your own interpretation.

We all want to be listened to and understood, although many of us do not actively participate in this process. The ability to listen to other people and to understanding what they are trying to tell us is an extremely important skill. When you improve your ability to listen, you will benefit from a positive change in your relationships and you will reap the rewards of a being known as a "good listener."

Offer Friendly Words

"Kind words can be short and easy to speak,
but their echoes are truly endless."

~Mother Teresa

Of all the gifts you can give to a dear friend, family member or even a stranger, a few kind words can often be the most poignant. Think about the philosophy behind the act of giving somebody a material item, whether it is a bunch of flowers, a car or only a can of soda. Assuming no ulterior motive, the sentiment is always the same. It's simply an expression of kindness – an attempt to spread a little joy.

Of course, it's impossible to claim a few magical words uttered now and then will turn life into a wonderful dreamland. However, a simple gesture to show someone you care can make a huge difference to that person's mood. In addition, some strong words of encouragement can make the difference between success and failure.

The effects of positivity as opposed to negativity

Even the most clichéd terms, such as "you can do it" or "do yourself proud" can have a profound effect on the way someone goes about their task. When a football team gets ready for a big game, the coach doesn't deliver a pep talk just for the sake of doing it. He or she knows that by giving the players that extra little bit of confidence the team will be stronger, tougher and more likely to win the day.

In Freudian psychology, there is a phenomenon known as 'displacement,' whereby a negative behavioral pattern or emotional state rubs off onto others. Here's an example of how displacement might work. An aggravated customer walks into a shop after recently being out in the heavy rain. He speaks to the shop owner in a harsh manner. The shop owner, in turn, is rude to the next customer who subsequently takes out their anger on a work colleague, and so on. This chain-reaction can go on for any amount of time, but if you're aware of it, then you can be the one who stops it from continuing.

The next time you're at the counter in your local store and the cashier is clearly in a bad mood, try doing the following. Look at them directly in the eye, smile, and say "Hi, how are you?" or something similar. Although if at first you may wonder why you bothered, keep smiling and maybe even say something encouraging or try to make them laugh. You'll see how quickly their mood changes and you'll realize that you've just made someone's day.

On the odd occasion that it doesn't work, for example when there is something seriously wrong and the person doesn't cheer up, at least you've offered them some friendly words. In addition, by becoming proactively positive you have prevented yourself from taking on their negative mood. In psychological terms, the stronger or more 'highly charged' emotion is the one that becomes dominant and transfers to other people, displacing its weaker counterpart. Therefore, your expression of positivity and happiness can essentially override the anger or sadness of another person.

This is particularly effective within a network of friends. Words of wisdom, advice, comfort and support from one friend to another can be far more potent than those between two strangers. The bond of trust between friends, as well as the mutual respect that goes with it, can add extra emotional weight to such expressions of kindness.

"To handle yourself, use your head;
to handle others, use your heart."

~*Eleanor Roosevelt*

Chapter 5

Live in Gratitude

"Be content with what you have, rejoice in the way things are.
When you realize there is nothing lacking,
the whole world belongs to you"

~Lao Tzu

Count the Blessings in Your Losses

"We cannot change the cards we are dealt,
just how we play the hand."

~Randy Pausch

*L*oss comes in many forms and it can be debilitating. Death may take a loved one. A breakup may take a lover. A job loss may take our livelihood. A financial collapse may take our home. Losses can be monumental or they may be small, but either way they can still be life-changing.

A loss is followed by periods of denial, anger and grief. After you allow yourself to experience all these emotions, the time comes to move past them and chart a course to go forward. It is also a time to take inventory of the blessings in your life.

It is said that you find out who your true friends are during your darkest hours. Sometimes those friends are the people you least expect. When you suffer a loss, certain people will emerge as protectors, consolers, providers and as an overall source of strength. The people who stand by your side during and after a loss are a golden find and the best kind of blessing. These are the friends who will comfort you and help you navigate through your troubled waters. They will continue to be by your side when the times are also good, so be sure to remember them when they experience a loss and need a friend.

Losing somebody
The loss of a friend or a loved one can leave a huge void in

both your life and your heart. It is difficult to find blessings when someone is taken away from us. But those blessings can be found in your memories of that person. Be thankful for the time you did share with them. Preserve those memories and help keep them alive for others, especially people who may not have had the opportunity to know them long enough or well enough to have solid memories of their own.

Losing a job

A job loss can shatter our confidence and self-esteem. We may feel unworthy and incapable of supporting ourselves or our families. On the other hand, a job loss can be turned into an opportunity to find the work we really want to do. Perhaps it is a good time to assess our skills and map out a plan to gain new ones or improve those that we currently have. This could mean heading back to school, finding an apprenticeship or signing up for career counseling to determine where we want to be and how to get there. When we redefine our purpose and take steps to achieve a new goal, the blessings will manifest themselves in our accomplishments and satisfaction.

Losing material possessions

A financial loss is also tough to swallow. In hard economic times, we must often give up material goods. Rather than lament over the things you can no longer have, find a new appreciation for the possessions in your life. Material things are just that – they do not define who we are and they should never be a priority. Giving up material possessions is a time to re-evaluate the things that are most important to us in life like friends, family, and good health. When we are forced to give up material possessions, it is amazing how we learn to live with so much less. We sometimes reach a point where we have to ask ourselves why we needed all those things in the first place. Were they taking the place of something that should hold higher importance? Were they filling a void? Use this time to adjust your living habits. Then the real blessing comes when you are able to get back on your feet, making the conscious decision to continue to live with less.

Blessings can be found in any situation where we incur a loss, but it takes soul-searching and fortitude to uncover them. Once you find your blessings, savor them and keep them close. The wonderful thing about blessings is that they multiply when you treasure them and share them with others who are in need.

Don't Let Heartbreaks Break You

"Never allow someone to be your priority
while allowing yourself to be their option."

~Mark Twain

What does not kill me makes me stronger. Those in the midst of suffering from a broken heart may say this quote from Frederick Nietzsche is hogwash. Those who have survived heartbreak will nod their heads in agreement.

Heartbreak can be the worst pain you ever experience in a lifetime. It can manifest itself in both physical and emotional ways. When you are hurting from a broken heart you may lose your appetite, become an insomniac, cry often, and find yourself unable to navigate your daily life. You may be plagued with anxiety and panic attacks that come on suddenly, leaving you unable to breathe, focus, or function. You may suffer bouts of uncontrollable crying, anger, or depression. And sometimes you may believe your life is over and the pain will never go away.

News flash! Your life is not over and the pain will go away. And during the healing process, you will make discoveries about yourself, your needs, and your desires. Most importantly, you will know the pitfalls to avoid so you never have to suffer this pain again. Heed these lessons from the school of heartbreak.

Limit your attendance to the pity party
Yes, you need to grieve. But there is a big difference between

releasing pain and wallowing in it. Misery does love company and those who have been wronged by a lover will welcome you into the fold. Allow yourself some limited visits inside the circle. Share your story, express your anger, cry on others shoulders, and embrace your pain. And then move on. Positive and negative energies are powerful, so you must make the conscious decision about which type you will choose to surround you. Connect with friends and family who are emotionally healthy and who will infuse you with love, warmth, confidence, and most of all, laughter.

Reassess your goals

There is always an underlying reason behind heartbreak, and contrary to what you may be thinking, it takes two to cause the demise of a relationship. Make a list of pros and cons about the failed relationship and then reassess the goals you want to achieve in a future relationship. It is not so much about what you want the other person to be, it is about the person you want to be when you are with them. The best relationships are those that allow you to shine in your own light.

Fall in love with yourself first

It is impossible to be happy with another person unless you are happy with yourself. Happiness should be a culmination of physical, mental, and emotional well-being. Before you begin the search for a new soul mate, give yourself a tune up. What parts of you became stale during the prior relationship? Are you eating healthy and getting exercise? Are you engaging in activities that stimulate your mind? Are you connecting with people who boost your self-esteem? Successful self-help means putting your needs first for a while. When you reach the point where you think you can be all that you can be, only then is the time right to allow yourself to once again be one-half of a pair.

Never settle for less

When you reach the point where you are ready to embark again on a relationship, proceed with caution. Don't try to fit a round peg in a square hole for the sake of completion. Finding a partner who is the right fit takes time. You know what you want, and more importantly, you deserve to have it. Don't settle for less than that, especially when the red flags pop up. Trust your instincts and your healed heart. They won't let you down.

The lessons you learn from your heartbreaks are important. If you study them, they will prepare you for the next venture into the relationship world. But like any lessons you learn, you must continually review them so you don't forget. Give yourself a Cliff Notes version and refer to it frequently!

Seek Daily Inspiration

"If you can dream it, you can do it."

~Walt Disney

*I*nspiration entails being in an ebb and flow of creativity and intellectual stimulation. Inspiration entails imagination and ingenuity. Inspiration is what allows us to get lost in a project for hours, paint a masterpiece, or write a beautiful piece of music. Inspiration can mean the difference between dragging yourself to the coffee pot in the mornings and springing out of bed like a kangaroo on steroids. Inspiration is what keeps us living and not just existing.

Finding inspiration
The beauty of it all is that you don't have to consider yourself an artist, musician or poet to seek inspiration daily. The truth is you are the painter, sculptor, writer and creator of your life. You – yes you – can live a life of inspirational magnitude.

You can find inspiration in the laughter of a child, in the breeze as it moves or in a cloud formation. You can find it in the smile of a stranger, the kindness of a neighbor or a letter from a friend. Inspiration can be found in the accomplishment of daily tasks, the hope of a new adventure or the memory of a loved one.

Daily inspiration becomes more of an allowing rather than a seeking - for it is all around us. We have only to open our eyes and hearts to see and feel inspiration. Inspiration may come through a quiet voice, a favorite song or a playful pet. We must learn to allow whatever form it takes. We must learn to acknowledge it when it comes, and to embrace it while it lasts. To help you on your journey, here are some things you can do to increase your awareness of those inspirational moments.

- Start doing. Paint, write, play and otherwise engage in life. There are no more excuses or waiting for the inspiration to come before you begin. Start and the inspiration will appear.

- Immerse yourself in experience. Find something you love to get involved in and watch as inspiration washes over you. Do you like to dance? Do it! Find a class and a partner, or get a video. Turn on your favorite music and shake what you've got. Do you love art and photography? Start a scrapbook club or exchange ideas with friends. Do you love plants? Volunteer at your city park or take a tour of a nearby nursery. If you don't already have a hobby or know what you love to do, try something new. Sometimes the best inspiration comes when you dare to step out of your comfort zone.

- Seek inspiration daily. You can find it in galleries and coffee shops, by the lake or in the garden. You can find it through people you admire, people you love to be with and through quiet time with yourself. You can find inspiration in books, magazines and movies. You can seek inspiration through both activity and meditation. Inspiration can come through silence or noise, busyness or stillness.

Inspiration can come through the small, cherished moments of daily living. It comes from doing something you love with people that are dear to your heart. It does not have to be anything earth shattering, and may not be a light bulb moment. Often flashes of inspiration come from ordinary things or events. It can be triggered by the nudge of your puppy's wet nose or your son's infectious laugh. The sight of a family heirloom or a line from a favorite book can trigger the most inspiring memories and moments. These are the treasures of a life well-lived. Pause and recognize them. Today, bask in the inspiration that is available in all you do and all you see. The world is waiting for you to find the inspiration you seek - so that others will feel it too.

Practice Gratitude

*"Acknowledging the good that you already have in your life
is the foundation for all abundance."*

~*Eckhart Tolle*

*S*o what is gratitude and how can we live by it, rather than only speak about it?

What is gratitude?

Gratitude is a state of being grateful, thankful, and appreciative. To live in a state of gratefulness is to be in a state of continual awareness of people, experiences, and objects you appreciate. Before we discuss how you can implement more gratitude into your life, let's take a look at how being grateful affects your brain.

Gratitude and your brain

According to gratitude researchers and psychologists Robert Emmons and Michael McCullough, weekly gratitude practices have a profound effect on both mind and body. Studies performed by these two researchers have found that those who consistently kept gratitude lists and journals exercised more regularly, were more optimistic, and had higher energy levels. Overall, grateful people were happier people. Scientists are only beginning to scratch the surface on the physiological effects of appreciation. Did you know your heart's electromagnetic field can be measured 8 to 10 feet from your body? This electrical energy of what you are thinking and feeling shows up in the brain waves of those who are close by us. Not only will an attitude of gratitude affect your own mind and body, but also those around you.

Implement more gratitude into your life

So what are some practical ways to implement more gratitude and appreciation into your daily life?

- Lists. Like the people in the study performed by Emmons and McCullough, you can keep a daily gratitude list or journal. How you choose to do this is completely up to you. Some prefer to write their lists in the morning before starting their day. Others prefer to recap their day's appreciations before bed. If you want to jump right into it, you could try both. Get a special notebook with a fun cover or make your own. Find an inviting chair and quiet place where you won't be disturbed. It only takes a few minutes and this practice can make an enormous difference in the way you feel. Pick a person that you love and list what you appreciate about them. Maybe you had a memorable experience recently of which you can write. Look around the room for small objects that you love to add to your list. Feel free to be creative and make the journal your own. After all, your notebook is for you and will help you recount all the glorious things happening in your life. Over time, you will be able to see how you have changed and grown.

- Pictures. If writing a daily list is not your speed, consider using pictures. With all the smart phone cameras now available, it is easy to take quick snapshots. You can capture a fun moment with friends, your child or pet's humorous antic of the day, or a gift that you adore. Keeping a digital album on your phone gives you the opportunity to browse and elevate those feelings of appreciation at any time throughout the day. If you don't have a phone with a camera you can put two or three pictures of things you love in your wallet. Take them out on occasion and focus on the wonderful feelings they conjure.

- Giving Back. Another great way to increase your sense of gratitude while helping improve the lives of others is through volunteering. With so many opportunities and organizations to choose from, you don't have to make substantial time commitments. Find something you are passionate about and use it as a way to give back. Write a letter to someone who could use a friend. Visit your local animal shelter or nursing home. Read a book to a child. Take a neighbor some baked goodies or flowers. It does not take much to make someone else smile. Taking the time to bring hope and laughter to another helps you appreciate all that you have and makes you feel warm and fuzzy inside.

These ideas represent a fraction of the ways to allow more gratitude into your life. Through daily practice of gratitude, you can make a difference not only in your life, but also in the lives of those around you. It only takes a few minutes a day to have a profound impact.

"As we express our gratitude, we must never forget that the highest appreciation is not to utter words, but to live by them."

~John F. Kennedy

Chapter 6

Share Yourself with Others

"Life isn't about finding yourself. Life is about creating yourself."
~George Bernard Shaw

Give More Than You Take

"Not all of us can do great things.
But we can do small things with great love."

~Mother Teresa

*O*ur core convictions concerning the nature of ourselves and what this existence is all about – our life philosophies – can impact our everyday choices in ways we seldom suspect. For example, if we see ourselves as an integral part of creation, and connected with everything else, then it can be easier for us to want to give to others. Giving becomes indistinguishable from receiving. If we see ourselves as separate and alone in a hostile universe then the idea of giving may seem unappealing and perhaps even foolhardy. We see giving as a way of letting go of our advantage. It's relinquishing a bit of the arsenal we're convinced we need in order to survive in a world that is "out to get us."

The latter philosophy has enjoyed a strong foothold in our world for a long time and it has caused a lot of loneliness, pain, selfish thought, and egocentric action. If we are to create a more nurturing environment for ourselves and for future generations then we must let go of such thinking. Finding a new paradigm that is more supportive and less destructive requires us to see past our own self-interest. We must understand that our fates are intertwined and that all life is connected. In essence, we do unto others what we do unto ourselves.

The wisdom in giving

Practicing generosity with our fellow human beings is a great way to grow into this new way of being. This practice encourages us to give more than we take. Oftentimes such a philosophy churns up fear within people if they believe making a habit of giving will have them winding up in the poorhouse or similarly disadvantaged. Energetically speaking, however, the reverse is true on a deeper level. A poverty mentality is what motivates us to cling to the things of this world or struggle for advantage. We imagine scarcity and thus, experience the same.

The urge to give comes from a totally different perception of reality. Generosity says, "This is a world of abundance. There's enough for everyone." Such thinking puts us in a position where our needs can be met by the universe.

If you give more than you take then your personal world is enriched. Trying to hoard whatever it is that you've managed to gain out of fear, a poverty mentality, or simple greed will cut you off from the flow of life. Not only will others not benefit from your generosity, but you will slowly become separated from the source of abundance.

What you give need not be monetary. You can give your attention to a lonely stranger. You can give advice to a younger person just starting out in your field of expertise. Generosity can be shown through your actions, your demeanor, your voice, and even your body language.

Giving more than we take can change the face of our world. This is the way of community, the way of the heart, and the way towards our ideal future. The spirit of generosity benefits all.

Support a Cause You Believe In

"Never doubt that a small group of thoughtful, committed citizens can change the world; indeed, it's the only thing that ever has."

Margaret Mead

*T*here are many causes, volunteer opportunities, and charities to which people can contribute. First let's talk about why it is important for you to find a cause to support in the first place. Supporting a cause allows you to give back to the world around you. Think about the blessings in your life and what you would like to share. The world needs your talents and abilities. As a remarkable individual, you present a unique contribution. Supporting a cause you believe in helps you expand your knowledge base and grow personally as well. Knowing that you are making a difference in the life of someone else is good for the soul. It helps you appreciate your own life more and often allows you to see the bigger picture. We tend to busy ourselves with daily tasks to the point that we forget what is important. Finding a cause to support can help you develop a healthier, happier perspective.

Finding a cause that resonates with you
With so many options to choose from, how do you find a cause that resonates with who you are and what you care about most?

Here are a few ideas:

- Evaluate your hobbies. Consider what your hobbies are. What is it that you do in your spare time? Do you have a pastime that you enjoy? Find a cause that supports that hobby. Maybe you have gained knowledge that you can share with others. Perhaps it has helped you develop skills that could be valuable in a charitable organization. Maybe a hobby peeked your interest in a particular area. Find a cause that aligns with the things you love to do.

- Ask yourself questions. Another option is to ask yourself some compelling questions. Questions can help you get to the core of your values. What are your passions? What do you want to contribute to your family, community, and the world? What do you care about most? What legacy do you want to leave? If you had all the time and money in the world, what would you contribute to and how? Questions help you evaluate where your priorities stand and what means the most to you.

- Find out what is available. Last but not least is to research your options. This can seem a bit overwhelming due to the vast number of charities and organizations. You don't have to evaluate every single one, however. After you have narrowed down what is important to you, it is time to do a little research. Search for a cause that is in line with what you value. When you find something that resonates with you, educate yourself. Find out what the cause is about, how it began, and its purpose.

How to be supportive

Once you have chosen a cause, you will need to figure out how you can contribute to and support it. There are many ways to do so - from financial contributions to volunteering of time and talent. Share your cause through social media, write letters, or hold fund-raisers. Rally other people who share your passions and get them involved too. Get creative. It does not have to take a lot of time and money to make a difference. Find something you are good at and enjoy doing. Use the talents you have and supporting a cause will not only warm your heart but bring joy to others, as well. For the benefit of yourself and the planet, find a cause you believe in.

"I don't know what your destiny will be, but one thing I know: the only ones among you who will be really happy are those who have sought and found how to serve."

- Albert Schweitzer

Give Of Your Time and Talents

"Generosity is giving more than you can,
and pride is taking less than you need."

~*Kahlil Gibran*

*W*hat do youth programs, hospitals, church ministries, community service organizations, humanitarian agencies, and most other non-profit groups have in common? They all depend on the support and participation of volunteers. In fact, without volunteers most of these organizations would cease to exist.

The advantages of volunteering

Serving as a volunteer holds obvious advantages for the organization, yet it also offers significant benefits for the volunteer. Consider these eight motivating factors:

*   Volunteering gives you an opportunity to give back to society. In some way, you have likely been on the receiving end of a volunteer organization already and by becoming a volunteer, you can make a positive impact on others.

*   Volunteering offers new challenges and opportunities. By volunteering, you can learn new skills while honing existing ones.

*   Volunteering is good for you mentally and physically. It keeps your mind and body active.

- Volunteering allows you to support a cause you believe in. Few activities are as fulfilling as volunteering in an area that is close to your heart.

- Volunteering lets you focus on your own interests. You get to choose where your energies and efforts will be directed.

- Volunteering provides social interaction. It's a vehicle for meeting new friends and developing relationships as you work toward shared goals.

- Volunteering puts your skills, wisdom, and experience into action. Rather than allowing life lessons to lie dormant, you can apply them in practical ways and pass them on to others.

- Volunteering produces the satisfaction of living beyond your own self. Serving can help you keep life in perspective as you respond to the needs of others.

So where do you start? To help you narrow down your volunteer options, ask yourself these questions:

- What causes and/or organizations matter to me?

- What abilities or experiences do I have to offer?

- Are there life skills I can teach to others?

- In what areas do I want to grow personally?

- How much time can I contribute?

- Where do my friends volunteer?

Reflecting on the answers to these questions may bring certain possibilities to the forefront. However, if you are still unsure, check with your local volunteer center or church. You may also discover additional opportunities in your newspaper's public service announcements or by searching online.

The "Baby Boomer" generation

While volunteering is an important activity for any age group, Baby Boomers are in a unique position. About a third of all of those in the Baby Boomer generation already volunteer in some capacity. With their own families already reared, and with less pressure to earn a living, Boomers have greater flexibility to invest their time in meaningful ways.

David Eisner, former CEO of the Corporation for National and Community Service, explained it this way: "America's Baby Boomers are an untapped resource of extraordinary proportions. They are the largest, healthiest, best-educated generation in history, and they can leave an incredible legacy through service to others."

Communicate with Love

"Being deeply loved by someone gives you strength,
while loving someone deeply gives you courage."

~Lao Tzu

*L*ydia burst through the door excited to tell Grandma about her day at school. Having won an award for exemplary behavior, Lydia was beyond excited to show Grandma. Sitting in a chair at eye level with Lydia, Grandma smiled and gave her a big hug and exclaimed enthusiastically, "I am so proud of you, Lydia." A gigantic smile crossed Lydia's face and warmed Grandma's heart.

This simple interaction has left both Lydia and Grandma feeling fulfilled, supported, and loved. It happened in a matter of minutes, but its significance goes far outside of mere words. So let's take a look at what really happened.

First, Lydia already knows she has Grandma's support. That is why she is so proud of herself, knowing Grandma will be, too. She feels safe and secure, knowing that Grandma will share her enthusiasm like she has so many times before. Grandma is such a valuable support in Lydia's life.

Next Grandma greets Lydia with openness and warmth. Soft eyes and a smile are all it takes to let Lydia know that Grandma's arms and heart are open to her. Grandma gets down to Lydia's level showing her that she truly cares about what Lydia has to say. Grandma listens intently as Lydia shares the important experience with her.

Grandma and Lydia share a hug, bringing the power of human touch to their interaction. Human touch is a power not to be under estimated. Touch strengthens relationships as well as soothes and calms. A simple hug or back rub, releases tensions, improves mood, and brings comfort.

Lastly, Grandma clearly tells Lydia how proud she is. Although they are important, it's not the words that have the most power. It's Grandma's expression and tone of voice. Grandma means what she is saying and is honestly enthusiastic about Lydia's accomplishments no matter how small they seem. Grandma's heart resonates with Lydia as they share a bond so significant to both their lives.

The importance of loving communication
The weight of honest, loving, and open communication in any relationship with a child is great. Its impact lasts from the developmental years of a toddler through those challenging teenage years and beyond. Communicating effectively with both young people and older people calls for interest and compassion. Talking with children without demeaning them or labeling them can at times be challenging. However, being able to express yourself to the children in your life openly and honestly is so important. It is far worth the time and effort it requires. In order to communicate effectively in a positive manner, you must begin with a mutual respect and understanding.

Telling a child you love them and meaning it impacts not only their mental well-being, but also physical well-being. Having the support of family gives children the courage they need to venture out into the world. It gives them a safe place from which to explore and expand their hearts and minds. If you have ever told a child you were proud of them and watched as their faces lit up, you know what a difference those simple words can make. Positive, loving communication is not about words only, but about how the words are presented and the realness that is felt within them. Do you honestly mean what you are saying? How is your tone of voice? What is your body language conveying? Are you not only speaking, but really listening? All these things together create the mood and feeling of an interaction. Every interaction you have with your child is either building or tearing down the bonds you are working to create. We all have days where we are not at our best. We all make mistakes and don't communicate in the positive way we would like. Negative interactions are going to happen from time to time. The important thing for children to know is that no matter what they are loved and supported.

You can communicate this through authentic praise, touch, and genuine listening. Whether a guardian, parent, or grandparent, remember not to take the interactions with children for granted. The relationship you are building will impact a child's ability to grow and respond to the world around him. Appreciating your children for who they are, where they are, and letting them know it will build a bond that cannot be easily broken. Children who experience interactions like these will have the courage they need to go out into the world and live lives of value and meaning.

*"All you need is love, but a little chocolate
now and then doesn't hurt"*

~Charles M Schulz

Chapter 7

Bring Joy Into Your Life

"Joy is what happens when we allow ourselves to recognize how good things really are."

~Marianne Williamson

Practice Appreciating Yourself

"Do you really want to be happy? You can begin by being appreciative of who you are and what you have."

~Benjamin Hoff

*I*t is human nature to want to feel appreciated. Everyone enjoys an "atta-boy" or "atta-girl" once in a while. Expressed appreciation serves as a confirmation of the value of some task we performed or an action we completed. It lets us know we performed well and we accomplished something worthwhile or our efforts were noticed.

Though acknowledgement is uplifting, we can get caught in a trap when we depend on others to shore up our self-esteem by expecting to be provided with a constant show of appreciation. If we become dependent solely on others to gauge our worth we may be setting ourselves up for disappointment. Sometimes others are caught up in their own issues, and even though they may be in awe of our deeds, they simply don't have the time or energy to express praise. We then feel under appreciated because we expected an accolade that didn't come.

No one understands the value of what you do more than you do. So why not allow that self-esteem boost to come from within? It takes some work and some practice, but the payoff is well worth it.

Make a list of your assets
If you are going to learn to appreciate yourself, you need to know

what you do well. Assets include talents, traits and aptitudes. Are you artistic? Are you athletic? Are you a good communicator? Are you a good listener, counselor, or problem solver? In what areas do you excel? What are the things you do in your everyday life which people often compliment you about? When you take the time to actually put these thoughts down on paper, you will be surprised at how many positive traits you have that you need to appreciate.

Focus in on your top achievements

Once you have assembled your list, choose the top five or six traits in which you believe you excel. Under each of those headings, list specific accomplishments of which you are the most proud. Perhaps you received a trophy in a sporting event or an academic award. Maybe it was the time you helped a friend in need. It could be recognition at work for a special project or even the attainment of a personal goal. Seeing your achievements in black and white gives them credence and substance. Keep this list as a reference and add to it each time you complete another worthwhile accomplishment. Read that list when you need a boost in your confidence and allow it to remind you of your outstanding capabilities.

Reward yourself

Don't wait for others to recognize your worth. Reward yourself for a job well done. Design a wish list and allow yourself to buy or obtain items on that list when you are feeling good about yourself. Whether it is a new outfit, a meal at a favorite restaurant, a mini-visit, or an extravagant vacation, give yourself the recognition you have earned. The good part about this process is that you never have to be disappointed with a gift if you pick it out and give it to yourself. Who knows better about what you want and need than you!

Never give up

Achieving a goal and recognizing your accomplishments is euphoric. But it should never be viewed as an end. You should continually be establishing new goals for yourself and continually sharpening the skill sets that will help you attain those new goals. Practice your musical instrument, increase the weights on your exercise machines, take enrichment classes, or perfect your hobbies. Take the advice often given in Army recruiting commercials that says, "Be all that you can be." The more you excel, the more you will appreciate the person you are and the closer you inch toward being the person you most want to be.

Self-appreciation is by no means selfish or egotistical. It is a realistic way to reward positive behavior. It doesn't mean you care less about others, it simply means you take the time and energy to care about yourself in a way that no one else can.

Practice Mindfulness

"Meditate. Breathe consciously. Listen. Pay attention.
Treasure every moment. Make the connection."

~*Oprah Winfrey*

As modern living becomes ever more stressful and demanding, people are looking for inspiration and advice on how to ease the strain of daily life. One concept that is gaining a lot of attention is "mindfulness." It sounds uplifting, but it is also somewhat vague.

What is mindfulness?
Mindfulness has its roots in Buddhism and is one of the seven factors of enlightenment according to the teachings of the Buddha. In short, it is a form of meditation in which one is encouraged to feel at peace with the world around them by paying attention to things they would not normally notice. This includes having a greater appreciation for various sights and sounds in nature, and even food and drink. Buddhists incorporate breathing exercises as a technique to attain mindfulness, and they feel that it helps them establish a sense of calm and tranquility.

However, if you cannot envision devoting yourself to Buddhism and scheduling regular meditation sessions throughout your day, there are still lessons to be learned about the positive effects of mindfulness. By taking more notice of your surroundings, sensations, and emotions in your everyday comings and goings, you can feel less stressed and develop a clearer state of mind.

Mindfulness can reduce stress

The typical Westerner's approach to eating and drinking is a pertinent example of how a lack of mindfulness can lead to fractured thinking and discomfort. Often, when having a meal, we are doing something else at the same time such as watching television, speaking to a colleague, or even working. We finish our meal feeling as though we haven't particularly enjoyed it, or worse, suffering from bloating and indigestion as a result of wolfing down the food too quickly. To be "mindful" when eating, you should remove yourself from distractions and pay full attention to the act itself. This does not mean simply having a solitary lunch in a quiet place; it involves purposefully paying attention to the tastes and textures of the food you are consuming, as well as your own responses to those sensations.

Mindfulness is a concept that places focus on the present rather than the past or future. This philosophy is in contrast with the values of Western society in which we are usually either fretting about something that has already happened or worrying about what is to come. This mind set means we miss out on a lot of life experience. For instance, when going out for a walk in the park, we may be plotting and planning in our heads, or analyzing what we could have done better at work or at home. By doing this, we fail to notice the splendor of the trees and flowers around us, the scents in the air, and how the light falls. Making the effort to notice these things, or being mindful, instantly relieves the stress of daily life, allowing us to feel more "in the moment."

Benefiting from mindfulness

Mindfulness is not simply another means of relaxation. It involves much more than simply closing your eyes and shutting out tedious thoughts for a few minutes. It is a process by which you can learn to develop a greater appreciation for the world at large, and it is definitely achievable by the average person. Thoughts about your tasks and chores will inevitably intrude, but as long as you refocus on the present, you will recapture mindfulness. The benefits of mindfulness are many. As well as obtaining a greater sense of calm, you will find that when it is once again time to consider work or relationship issues, your mind will be less strained from over-analysis, and therefore able to devote itself more effectively to the task at hand.

Research on the benefits of mindfulness is ongoing but brain scans have shown a reduction in stress for those who practice it, and even relief in discomfort levels for patients suffering from ailments such as chronic back pain. To observe examples of the favorable effects of mindfulness, however, all you need to do is look at some of the world's happiest people: children. Children are masters of "staying in the moment." Whether playing outside, eating, or taking a bath, they notice and respond to their experiences. They might comment on how the grass feels against their skin or how the sound of the water gurgles.

Being mindful is showing a full appreciation of our environment rather than relegating it to the background while we contemplate mundane things. This technique can change your approach to life and immeasurably improve your health.

Practice Peace in Your Life

"Guard well within yourself that treasure - kindness.
Know how to give without hesitation, how to lose without regret,
how to acquire without meanness."

~*George Sand*

*I*nside of each of us lies an entire world woven out of our thoughts and feelings, both conscious and unconscious. This world can be a source of joy, insight, and wisdom as well as a source of pain, darkness, and delusion. Many mystics, shamans, and philosophers the world over – and even many quantum physicists in the modern day – have maintained that the outer world we experience is a reflection of a person's inner world.

This means we are collectively responsible for our wars, as well as for our times of peace. Our inner conflicts feed our external ones. By the same token, when we find harmony within ourselves – when we are able to practice peace in our personal lives – we contribute to world harmony.

How do we practice peace?
To practice peace in our lives, we must first know ourselves and become acquainted with any disturbing influences we're carrying inside. We have to become conscious of them, so instead of projecting them into our daily environment and the larger world situation, we can accept them as thoughts and feelings that belong to us but do not define us. This kind of self-acceptance brings our personal power back into our court. If we're not identified with these negative influences, or erroneously mistaking them for

the realities of the world, then we can begin to let them go.

Self-awareness and inner peace

It can be very difficult to practice peace in our interactions with others if we have wounds, buried disappointments, resentments, and hidden fears that we haven't acknowledged within ourselves. We'll be too vulnerable and prone to being triggered by the words and actions of others. Our reactions – the source of which can remain a mystery to us – will continually disrupt any sense of tranquility that we may have managed to create for ourselves.

Self-awareness, on the other hand, allows us to practice peace consciously every day of our lives. Having forgiven ourselves, we're able to forgive others. Having found compassion for ourselves, we're better able to express compassion towards the people that we meet.

Methods of cultivating peace

There are two methods you can utilize to help order your inner environment and thus enable you to practice peace in your life. The first approach works on a feeling level. The next time you find yourself in the grips of a powerful emotional reaction, sit for a while with the emotion itself instead of venting or otherwise acting it out in the world. Oftentimes, destructive emotions can be covering up deeper feelings that are hard to face. Anger may be covering up some deeper fear, or depression may be blanketing pain. We can only hear the messages such deeper feelings have for us if we resist the temptation to react, and instead remember that our feelings are our own to work with.

The other approach is mental. Take some time every day to listen objectively to your own inner monologue. Do you notice fearful, limiting, or otherwise detrimental thoughts regularly running through your mind like negative mantras? These refrains are disrupting your inner harmony and preventing you from bringing peace into your life. Oftentimes you may find these mantras lose their power over your mind when they are identified. The daily inner suggestions we give ourselves can seem ridiculous once we voice them aloud, but they hold a lot of weight if we consider them statements of truth and never examine them.

Both of these methods will get you better acquainted with your internal environment and help you to practice peace in your personal life – and, hopefully, to touch the lives of others with your peaceful presence.

Practice Being Happy

*"Happiness is something you are and it comes
from the way you think"*

~Wayne Dyer

*H*appiness is defined by Webster's dictionary as a state of being content. This can be misleading, however. Using that definition, it sounds like a state you are either in or you're not in. While there is some truth to the definition, happiness is actually a state of mind you can create within yourself. You do not have to rely on circumstances or wait for the winds of change to bring about a state of happiness. Happiness is not something that occurs on a whim, though sometimes it seems that way. Happiness is a state that can be cultivated through practice.

Choosing happiness

The benefits of practicing happiness are numerous and far reaching. Happy people are healthier, wealthier, more fulfilled, and content with their lives. Happy people live with an energy that seems to attract more good things to them. Others may look upon this with the idea that these people are lucky and blessed. But this is not always the case. Some of the happiest people have gone through the most trying circumstances. The difference, however, is in the choices that they have made in their lives. Rather than thinking that the world is out to get them, they have chosen to view the world as a loving place. They have made a decision, whether conscious or unconscious, to look for the beauty in the world around them. They have chosen happiness. Therefore they feel happiness.

Choosing happiness in spite of circumstances can be challenging at first. Changing your thoughts and feelings can take a little time. However, it is time well spent. As you work to change the thought patterns that rattle through your head on a daily basis, you can literally change the way you feel. Take a moment right now to think of a time you were really happy. Who were you with? What were you doing? Now immerse yourself in that memory. What sights do you see? What do you smell and hear? Intentionally elevate those good feelings. Let the memory wash over every part of your being. Now how do you feel? Did you feel your energy and mood rise?

As a human being, you are meant for happiness. And at your core, you are aware of this. That's why you feel so miserable when you focus on the things that keep happiness from you. You are an amazing being that has the ability to carry happiness within no matter what is going on without. Why would you choose anything else?

Practicing happiness
If happiness is a practice, we must first make the decision to practice it. Now granted, making that decision is easier said than done. There is something to the old saying, "fake it until you make it." This is not to say you must continually pretend and never be real with those around you. But try putting a smile on your face and see what a difference it makes. That act alone can raise your vibration and attract others that are also feeling good.

Here are a few more suggestions:

- Take a little time to compile a list of things that make you happy. Your list can consist of items like a walk in the sunshine, listening to your favorite song, or viewing a picture of a pet or grandchild. Write this list on an index card and keep it with you. Take it out when your mood needs a boost. To the list add a few special memories that elevate your feelings when you think about them.

- Do something you love every day. Learn to enjoy the simple things life brings. Chew your food slowly and bask in the deliciousness of your meal. Stop to look at the intricate detail of a wild flower by the sidewalk.

- Make a daily list of three to five things for which you are immensely grateful.

When you find yourself thinking negative thoughts that don't serve you, stop and ask yourself how it is affecting your mood. Accept the thought for what it is, realize it is your old pattern of thinking, and change it to one that feels better.

Over time, your thought patterns will begin to change. You will find that you no longer have to constantly monitor your thoughts, because they have grown more positive. You will find that you have a better outlook on life. And you will soon find that you are more appreciative and have happiness radiating from within.

Laugh at Yourself and the World

"A day without laughter is a day wasted."

~Charlie Chaplin

*W*hat do lower blood pressure, boosted immunity, less stress and tighter relationships have in common? The answer believe it or not is laughter. Could it be that laughter is the best medicine? When we take time to laugh at ourselves, we give ourselves permission to release tension and not take things too seriously.

Picture this: a man laughs hysterically as he enters the office, shoes in hand. When asked why he is arriving at work late and with no shoes on his feet, he recounts with humor the morning's events of puddles and taxis. His coworkers laugh along with him at his hilarious but unfortunate series of events. As the man proceeds to dry off his shoes, the whole office is laughing. The mood has risen for the day, and workers carry on their tasks with a renewed sense of relaxation and fun.

Now picture another man who has experienced a morning of similar events. Dragging into the office with shoes sloshing out water, he dares coworkers to even ask what happened. He proceeds to lock the door to his office and slouches down in his chair muttering under his breath. With tensions rising, everyone returns to their work hoping to avoid any more unpleasant confrontations for the day.

Which man do you think is going to have a better day? The answer is obvious. Not only will the man in the first story have a better day, but so will those around him. The truth is our moods and attitudes not only affect ourselves, but others as well. We need to learn to laugh at ourselves more. Things happen and sometimes they are inconvenient and even downright annoying. The ability to laugh at yourself and the world around you can actually change not only the kind of day you have, but your life.

Now I realize that sounds like quite a claim. Laughter can change my life? Indeed it can, and here is why:

1. Laughter has physiological benefits. From lowered blood pressure to better circulation, laughing does a body good. Anyone who has had a vigorous belly laugh can tell you that laughing puts those abdominal muscles to good use. Stress hormones such as adrenaline and cortisol are decreased while feel good hormones are increased.

2. Laughter brings people together. Others are naturally drawn to those that know how to have fun and laugh. Flashing a genuine smile and joining in on a joke shows you don't take yourself too seriously. Experiencing the joy of a humorous moment together bonds you will family and friends building stronger relationships.

3. Laughter is fantastic for the brain. Keeping your mind young and sharp, laughter increases creativity while using both left and right hemispheres. Adopting a more optimistic and amusing outlook can also ward off stress and depression. In addition, alertness is increased and memory improved.

How can you implement more laughter into your life? There are many ways to do so, and if you tend to lean on the pessimistic side of life a complete change is not likely to happen overnight. With practice, however, finding something to smile or laugh about every day will become easier. Here are a few ways to implement more fun and laughter into your life:

- The internet can be an excellent resource to find something that amuses you. From entertaining You Tube videos to amusing stories and pictures, you are sure to find something funny at any time of day.

- Play with your pet.

- Play with your children.

- Spend more time with your family.

- Watch a funny movie or television show.

- Go see a comedy act.

- Think about something you loved to do as a child and give it a go.

- Subscribe to a joke-a-day email or calendar.

Whatever you do, make laughter a priority in your life. Audrey Hepburn was on to something when she said, "I love people who make me laugh. I honestly think it's the thing I like most, to laugh. It cures a multitude of ills. It's probably the most important thing in a person."

So go have a good laugh today.

"Life is worth living as long as there's a laugh in it."
~LM Montgomery, Anne of Green Gables

Chapter 8

Love More Freely

"Love and compassion are necessities, not luxuries.
Without them humanity cannot survive. "

~Dalai Lama

Forgive Someone
(You Thought You Could Never Forgive)

"To forgive is to set a prisoner free
and discover that the prisoner was you."

~Lewis B. Smedes

There are many components to healthy human interactions such as trust, communication skills, and mutual respect. Forgiveness, however, is another critical aspect of good relationships that is often overlooked. By not practicing the art of forgiveness, people begin a process of grudge-building that fuels a powerful scourge that can quickly become an all-consuming plague in a person's psyche. Have you ever been around an older person who may have trouble remembering the day of the week but can recite every wrong ever done to them? This is a prime example of a life lived behind the iron bars of unforgivingness.

What is forgiveness?
Many people are reluctant to forgive because they have misconceptions about what forgiveness means and what it entails. They think that forgiveness is forgetting or tolerating indiscretions done at a personal level. Some believe that forgiveness is excusing malicious acts or somehow letting perpetrators "off the hook." On the contrary, forgiveness is not a courtesy extended to somebody else; instead, it is a great service that is done for one's own benefit. Forgiveness can be described as forbearing or forgoing the wrongdoing of another person in order to allow you the ability to move past indiscretions and entertain positivity

instead of being trapped in a bitter pit of negativity.

How to forgive

Depending on the degree of the wrong done against you, it may be harder to forgive some people than others, but the steps are essentially the same.

- Define the object of your forgiveness. Identifying who you need to forgive and why you need to forgive them will give you the basis for releasing the negative attachment you have to them. Write down the details of the matter if necessary, and be clear in articulating exactly what the offense was or is.

- Feel your negative feelings. Forgiveness is not a call to deny or repress feelings. It is a process by which you work through any negative emotions harbored against other people. There are many ways to accomplish this task. Again, journaling offers a way to release your feelings and get them out of your internal environment. Somewhat like mental housekeeping, writing down your heartfelt emotions can be a very healing practice. Alternatively, talk therapy with a counselor, life coach, or pastor can often be of great benefit. In certain circumstances, it may even be appropriate to confront your perpetrator directly. The goal is to express your anger, resentment, and sadness in a constructive manner, thereby releasing the hold these negative feelings have over you.

- Adjust your perspective. Choose to forgive for your benefit, not anybody else's. When you are bound to your perpetrator with the cords of bitterness, you are choosing to self-inflict unnecessary heaviness upon yourself that is toxic to your psychological and physical well-being. Making the choice to forgive automatically releases the chains of negativity and allows you to experience peace and freedom in your life.

Forgiveness is an art form that takes courage to initiate and practice to perfect. It is not always comfortable to face the deep-seated emotions that are wreaking havoc in our lives, but living a life of forgiveness pays great dividends in the end.

Appreciate the Differences in Each Person

"If you judge people, you have no time to love them."
~Mother Teresa

One of the most detrimental things we can do in life is compare ourselves to others or try to imitate them. There will almost always be a negative bias in that sort of thinking. What's more, those thought patterns are based upon an illusion because this journey of life from the spiritual perspective is all about becoming more deeply ourselves. No one can be "more you" than you! So why waste time making comparisons? Why not honor your own uniqueness?

Throughout our entire history our differences have enriched the human experience. "Celebrate diversity" is a worthy credo for our times. Appreciate the differences in each person and you will come to know more fully how gifted, unique, and irreplaceable are every member of the human race.

The value in differences
All people play an essential role in creating the unique spirit of the times in which they live. For the sake of harmony and in the pursuit of peace in the world, it has been helpful for us to try to acknowledge our shared humanity – the common ground between us. Unity makes life possible for us, but diversity makes it more interesting and meaningful. Our differences grant us each the space in which to be ourselves and develop our individual gifts. In fact, nothing inspires men and women to achieve more

than their unique qualities. Because you are different you are here to fulfill a destiny that no one else can. Follow your personal path and in so doing you will appreciate the differences in the people all around you. We all have new things to contribute to this melting pot we call humanity.

One reason why many of us can fall prey to disinterest, apathy, and even depression is because we believe we've exhausted the possibilities of the world. There is nothing new; it has all been said and done. This sense is a fallacy, however, that grows in us when we're too stuck in our own habitual thoughts, attitudes, and habits. If you take the time to appreciate the differences in other people then you expose yourself to fresh perspectives, ideas, and beliefs that can broaden your horizons. There are as many ways of viewing the world as there are people within it and you never know when someone might share with you a fresh perspective that enables you to see your own life, with all its struggles and joys, in a new light.

A world where everyone is free to be different
Of course, such open-mindedness makes a positive impact in the world as well. Many of the conflicts between nations and most of our incidents of religious strife are not caused by any personal enmity that exists between people. They are, instead, generated by intolerance towards creeds, practices, traditions, and spiritual beliefs that differ from one's own. The human race needs increased tolerance and compassion if it is to continue into a sane and nurturing future. Appreciate the differences in each person and you'll be making your own personal contribution to world harmony.

This can be done in a multitude of ways. The crucial thing is to be mindful of your own attitudes and emotional responses when you interact with others. When someone expresses an opinion that strongly differs from your own notice the part of you that wants to close down or react. Then do these things instead:

- Listen with an open mind and discover whether there's something you can learn from the other person.

- Express your own opinion without judgment.

- Take the opportunity to learn about the other person without automatically allowing their words to reflect back upon your and your beliefs.

View the opinions and perspectives of others as part of the unique path they are travelling. Freedom can never die in our world so long as there are individuals living in it. Accept your own uniqueness and you will find it easy to appreciate the differences in each person you encounter upon life's journey.

Be a True Friend

"Friendship is born at that moment when one person says to another -
I thought I was the only one."

~*C. S. Lewis*

*T*rue-blue friends enrich our lives. They make the good times more enjoyable and the tough times more bearable. Being a faithful friend isn't always easy and doesn't happen overnight. Instead, it is a skill that requires constant attention and nurturing. A true-blue friend practices these basic concepts.

1. Place friendship at high priority in your life. Spend time with your friend. If your schedule is overloaded and you have little time to spare, a quick phone call or a text or email reminds your friend that you're thinking of her. As soon as you can, spend quality time with your friend, doing something you both enjoy.

2. Give your friend your undivided attention. Listen openly without trying to fix every problem. Listen without judging and don't offer opinions unless you're asked.

3. Be sensitive. It's important to offer help if you think your friend is going through a difficult time. Be there for your friend during the good times and the bad, even when it isn't easy or comfortable.

4. Reach out. Ask for help and support from your friend when you're the one who's struggling. By allowing your friend to be there for you, your friendship will grow stronger and more meaningful.

5. Be positive and upbeat. It's good to share problems and difficult times with your friends, but endless whining and complaining is an emotional drain and a good way to lose a friend.

6. Forgive. If your friend makes a mistake or hurts your feelings, talk about it and then let it go. True-blue friends don't harbor bitterness or resentment.

7. Apologize. If you've done something to offend or hurt your friend, admit it and make amends.

8. Be happy for your friend. Share in his accomplishments and successes, even if you feel envious or jealous.

9. Express genuine interest in your friend. Ask about things that are important to her such as her job, family, school, or hobbies.

10. Be loyal. Never belittle your friend to his face or put him down behind his back. Never gossip or tell things your friend has told you in confidence. Stick up for your friend if others are critical.

11. Give your friend space. Being a true friend doesn't mean you must spend every moment together. Don't be insecure and demanding and don't suffocate your friend. Allow her time for herself and time for other friends and other interests. Respect her privacy.

12. Agree to disagree. True friends aren't required to agree on everything. Respect your friend's difference of opinion because differences make life interesting and allow opportunities for learning. Turn conflicts and disagreements into give and take situations where you both benefit. If tempers flare, change the subject.

True-blue friendship is a two-way alliance consisting of constant give and take, but the rewards are well worth the effort. True-blue friendships are often lifelong arrangements that grow more meaningful with each passing year.

Keep in Touch with Those You Love

"Be a rainbow in someone else's cloud."

~Maya Angelou

*T*here was a time when communicating with loved ones who lived far away could take months, if it were even possible at all. Today, however, at the press of a button you can be in touch with someone living on the opposite side of the globe. The technology is there, so why is it that so many people still fail to keep in touch?

Maintaining contact with people in your own backyard can be difficult, so it is no wonder people often drift apart over vast distances. To prevent this from happening in your relationships, be intentional while using the tools at your disposal. Consider these suggestions:

1. **Put it on your calendar.** The opportunity to make a call or send an email may not come if you expect to do it "when you have a chance." Carve out time on your schedule—daily or weekly—for maintaining those connections.

2. **Be content with brief exchanges.** Composing volumes of text or gabbing for hours may sound ideal, but good intentions don't matter if they never actually become reality. If you only have 10 minutes, that's okay. Short but regular is better than long but rare.

3. **Use online video messaging.** Platforms such as Skype and FaceTime make it both easy and inexpensive to talk face-to-face,

even when separated by thousands of miles.

4. Take advantage of Facebook and Twitter. Post your thoughts and pictures so your friends and family can track you in real-time. Though these tools can never replace one-on-one interaction, they can help keep your connections intact.

5. Start a blog. Whether you use it to record your daily activities or to express your profound philosophies, a blog enables you to share your personal perspective while allowing others – including friends and family – to share the journey with you.

6. Redeem moments often wasted while waiting for others. Instead, take advantage of those few moments here and there to make a call or send a text or an email.

7. Don't forget traditional methods of communication. The occasional greeting card, newsletter, or snail mail letter may not be necessary, but it is often appreciated. Keep track of mailing addresses and put them to use at least once a year.

Keeping in touch is not difficult. In fact, it's easier than ever. It takes intentionality, however, and it does not happen by accident. You must purposefully prioritize maintaining your relationships.

The rewards you reap will make you glad you did.

*"Much unhappiness has come into the world because
of bewilderment and things left unsaid."*

~Fyodor Dostoevsky

Chapter 9

Be True to Yourself

"Be yourself — everyone else is already taken"
~Oscar Wilde

Practice Honesty on a Daily Basis

"If you tell the truth,
you don't have to remember anything."

~Mark Twain

*W*e've all heard the old adage: "Honesty is the best policy." And honesty is valued by all whether people like to admit it or not. Think about the last time you found out somebody wasn't completely honest with you. Chances are you experienced anger or disappointment, or maybe you even felt hurt and betrayed. Even though you may dislike dishonesty in others, it's interesting how we tend to regularly fall back on it, almost by default, when we don't want to face the consequences of a situation. For example, some people may embrace less-than-honest business practices in order to make a few extra dollars. Or, maybe telling the truth would open up a "can of worms" we aren't prepared to deal with in a personal relationship. Whatever the reason, being dishonest can affect many aspects of your life. On the other hand, practicing honesty builds character, strengthens relationships, and enhances a person's credibility.

Why incorporate honesty into your daily routine?
To answer that question, we have to ask another question first: If being honest is so beneficial, why do people often default to dishonest behavior? The answer lies in the human brain.

Dishonesty stems from fear – fear of consequences, fear of

being vulnerable, and fear of abandonment. The emotions of fear, lust, anger, and pleasure can be detected in the limbic system of the human brain through the use of electrodes. One way to conceptualize the limbic system is to think of it as a mechanism for "feeling and reacting." Interestingly, we share these same base emotions with all other animals that possess limbic systems. However, higher emotions such as unconditional love, honesty, courage, and compassion cannot be found in the limbic system. Instead, these emotions are found only in our larger, well-developed cerebrums.

Many people have a hard time experiencing a higher-order emotion such as honesty because they are living in a constant state of limbic reaction. Honesty depends on utilizing the capability of our higher order function, and practice is the only way to develop it.

Daily practices
To allow the benefits of honesty to permeate our lives, we must consciously practice it. Here are some ways to implement honesty in your daily life:

- Practice taking responsibility. The bare naked fact is that everybody must face the consequences of his or her actions. We can all summon a mental picture of a child with a face full of chocolate telling his mother he didn't eat the candy. He lies because he fears retribution. The fact of the matter is we all make mistakes and we all fall short of perfection. Make it a practice to own up to any and all actions that are yours. Eventually, you will find yourself making better choices and the temptation to lie in certain situations will diminish.

- Practice being fair. Although honesty is about using your words to tell the truth to others, and using your thoughts to be honest with yourself, it is also about action and behavior. We tell our children to play fair, but how many times do we find ourselves trying to beat the system?

How many times have you knowingly skated by on your taxes? The best policy when it comes to living an honest life is to follow your own advice and play fair. Give your employees a fair wage, pay your taxes according to law, and don't take the pens home from the office. They don't belong to you.

- Practice not making excuses. Excuses are often used as convenient justifications for doing things that are unethical, or sometimes they are used for avoiding responsibility. And, again, they stem from fear. You may feel like you have to come up with a reason for your decision as a way to avoid somebody being upset with you. Frequently excuses are thinly veiled words that attempt to hide deception. Be honest about why you say or do things. People will gain a better understanding of who you are, and you will earn greater respect in the process.

- Practice assertiveness. Many people don't feel like they can say what they really mean. And when they do, it can come off as, well – nasty. Assertiveness is the ability to diplomatically let other people know how you feel and where you stand without denigrating or belittling their character or opinions. Many people are not assertive because they are afraid of being criticized or ostracized. But being assertive involves being honest about how you feel and expressing that in a respectful manner. At first, it may feel uncomfortable, but with practice, it becomes second nature.

- Practice keeping your word. Oftentimes, promises are made without thinking and sometimes they are made because we don't want to make someone else angry by refusing their request. But the fact is your word is a precious commodity. And people can tell a lot about your integrity and your moral character by how well you keep your word. Don't agree to undertake tasks you know you cannot complete. If you commit to a project, do it faithfully.

Becoming more honest with yourself and others entails confronting the fears that drive you towards the tendency to deceive. As you cultivate more honesty into your life, you will find that people are instinctively drawn to you and trust you.

Honesty and integrity are the foundational elements of human civilization. For it is these values that allow us to reap the rewards of hard work, strong relationships, and strong character.

Express Yourself

"When people don't express themselves,
they die one piece at a time."

~*Laurie Halse Anderson*

Children should be seen and not heard. Many of us grew up believing in this proverb because our parents preached it to us. Girls were often told that ladies should be demure, unassuming and quiet – a sign of class and good manners. And men are often accused of not expressing their feelings because – well, because they are men.

The truth is that the expression of feelings is healthy for the body, mind and soul. It releases stress, aids communication, and helps make the world go around. There are a variety of ways to express your feelings, whether they relate to you or to another individual.

Expression through speaking

Speaking is the most common method of expressing your feelings, as well as the most readily available. Articulating your feelings in words can be liberating, and it can also be a vehicle for clarification. In today's technological world of emails and texting, the context of a message is often lost. As an example, speaking to another individual in person or on the telephone gives you the ability to express your honest and deep compassion when offering some form of consolation, a feeling not easily expressed in a written message on your phone or computer.

The inflection in your voice also lets everyone know if you are happy, sad, angry or bored. If you want your speech to be an effective expression of your feelings, take a deep breath before the words escape. This can be the difference between ending up with your foot in your mouth, or trying to take back words you did not intent to share.

Expression through action

Actions speak louder than words, or so the saying goes, as an action requires forethought and planning. Actions can be the ultimate way to express feelings toward another person. It can be an act of kindness to a neighbor or spending time with an elderly relative. It is showing affection to a partner or tenderness to a child. It can be baking a cake to celebrate something special or sending a bereavement card to console. Whatever action you take, the end result expresses an emotion that you were feeling at the time of the action.

Don't forget that you also need to express the emotions you are feeling about yourself. Reward yourself when you are proud of an accomplishment; pamper yourself when you need a boost; and allow yourself to grieve when you are upset or have suffered a loss. Being stoic has its place, but there are times you need to express those innermost feelings. It helps you to remember you are human.

Physical activity can liberate many feelings, especially uncomfortable ones. If you are feeling anxious, panicky or depressed, physical activity will increase blood flow, raise your heart rate, encourage deep breathing and, best of all, release endorphins. Walking, running, working out in the gym or taking out frustration on a punching bag are all beneficial ways to express emotions.

Expression through writing

Writing is an effective way to express a range of feelings. To journal or keep a regular diary serves to preserve memories as well as put your feelings on paper.

Writing when happy creates a story you can refer back to when your spirit needs rejuvenation. Writing when lonely creates a sense of purpose and helps you to appreciate those times when you are surrounded by family, friends, and loved ones. It is cathartic and provides an outlet for releasing unhappy emotions. If you can pour the unhappy emotions out on paper, you give yourself the opportunity to drain it from your soul to make room for happier, healthier emotions. Writing when angry is therapeutic and allows you to express those feelings in a non-threatening way.

One benefit of expressing your feelings through writing is that you can put it on paper when the feelings are raw. Then you can sleep on it and read it again after some time has elapsed. This can help you decide if you want to share those words with anyone else. If you are ambivalent, tuck them away for safe keeping.

Accept Yourself as You Are

*"Self-esteem comes from being able to define the world in your own
terms and refusing to abide by the judgments of others."*

~Oprah Winfrey

*M*any people equate self-acceptance with self-esteem and
although they are related, they are not quite the same. Simply put,
self-esteem refers to how valuable we perceive ourselves to be.
To have high self-esteem is to be able to specifically highlight our
respectable and admirable qualities.

On the other hand, self-acceptance is a broader concept that
embraces all aspects of self – failures and flaws included. By
learning to accept ourselves the way we are, we learn a lesson in
unconditional love. We recognize our faults and limitations, but
we are able to move past them in loving acceptance.

We start out accepting ourselves
Go back to your earliest memory. Chances are you can remember
back far enough to a time when self-acceptance was not an issue.
Children start out accepting themselves for who they are. Over
time, however, children begin to accept themselves in direct
relation to how their parents accept them.

Under normal circumstances, parents send positive and negative
messages based on how their children act. Quite naturally
and appropriately, we come to understand some behavior is
unacceptable and some is not. Conscious parents, however, are

133

careful to make sure that their children understand that just because an action is unacceptable or inappropriate doesn't mean that the person is any less loved.

Because many parents are not aware of this distinction, they tend to be overly critical, or even emotionally abusive. In these cases, the child will begin to foster feelings of inadequacy because he identifies himself with the offensive behavior. Not knowing any better, the child comes to accept the parent's negative assessment as valid. Repeatedly, the child continues to internalize painful feelings of rejection and the resulting belief that is carried into adulthood is that he is acceptable only under certain conditions. In essence, the young adult will "parent" themselves in much the same way they have been parented. Interestingly, psychologists have identified this critical, judgmental attitude toward oneself as a foundational element for a large portion of adult psychological suffering.

The pathway to self-acceptance

Ideally, everybody would grow up in a supportive, positive environment that nurtures self-acceptance. But as we all know, this is often not the case. So what if you are not one of these fortunate ones? The first thing to learn and teach others is you have the ability and the right to approve of yourself. Understand it is okay to think of yourself positively – even in spite of your shortcomings. After that, here are some tips for coming to a place of self-acceptance

- Exercise compassion. To people who are not accepting of themselves, compassion does not come easily, so following a directive to "have more compassion for yourself" is next to impossible. These people must start outside of themselves. When you begin to have compassion for others, you will begin to change your internal environment and compassion for yourself will come easier. A great way to foster compassion is to volunteer at an animal shelter, a soup kitchen, or at your child's school.

- Stop trying to be good enough. People who lack self-acceptance find themselves in an infinite loop of performing approval-seeking behavior as they try to meet the conditions they believe demonstrates their worthiness. Practice feeling okay not pleasing others. Go into life situations knowing not only should you not try to make everybody happy, but it would be impossible to do so even with your best efforts.

- Utilize affirmations. Replace your negative, critical inner dialogue with positive affirmations such as *In spite of my mistakes, I am worthy of love*. Or, *I am perfect the way I am*. You may not believe it at first, but over time you will accept your positive statement as truth. Remember, it took much repetition for you to agree to the negative belief. The good news is you can use the same process for installing positive beliefs.

Ultimately, self-acceptance is the act of laying down harsh judgment and self-criticism and learning to love yourself unconditionally. Self-acceptance leads to a new state of being – a natural state of happiness. In fact, many would say that happiness and self-acceptance are contingent upon each other. It is within your right to have peace of mind and personal fulfillment. Learning the art of completely accepting yourself will guide you down that path.

Live a Life True to Yourself
(Not the Life Others Expect of You)

"Those who mind don't matter,
and those who matter don't mind."
~Bernard M. Baruch

*W*e spend much of our life acting in ways that are meant to please others – our boss or coworkers, our friends, our spouse or significant other, our children, or our parents. The list goes on forever. But the only way to be content and fulfilled is to be true to ourselves. Of course, this task is easier said than done.

Our lives are often lived for others
It is easy to get caught up in our day-to-day routine and lose sight of who we really are and who we want to be. At work, we strive to please bosses, clients, customers, vendors and coworkers. At home, we often put our own needs aside in our attempts to grant the wishes of a spouse or our children. How often do we swallow our pride and act differently in order to boost the self-confidence of a friend or a significant other? Why do we feel the need to create an alter-ego for ourselves to keep someone else's super-ego from being bruised?

Living a life true to ourselves may seem foreign at first, but if we continually reinforce our good habits, eventually it will come naturally.

Becoming true to yourself
Depending on the type of work we do, we may swim in a sea

of rules, regulations and the corporate way of doing things. Though it is important to be a team player and put our company's needs in the forefront, there are times our personal ethics may be challenged. If moving forward with a work request goes against your grain, don't ignore those instincts. In many cases, a compromise can be worked out if you explain the situation to the powers that be. In extreme cases, you may be faced with a tough decision about your future with the company, but putting your own truths and beliefs aside in favor of the almighty dollar could leave you emptier emotionally than financially. Of course if push comes to shove and you find it is time to stand up for your principles, remember the movie Norma Rae. Get out your sign, stand on the desk, and chant your philosophy. You may end up looking like a hero to those around you.

When it comes to our families, it seems we justify putting our own needs on the back burner in order to ensure the happiness and well-being of our loved ones. As admirable as this gesture may be, there is a burnout point that can sneak up on you without warning. Caring, protecting, and nurturing a spouse, children, parents and other loved ones is an important task that requires attention. But unless we take care of ourselves first, we can't properly take care of anyone else. So before you take on the problems, issues, needs, or desires of others, be true to yourself by fulfilling your own needs and desires. Once you are emotionally, physically and mentally healthy, caring for others will not be a burden. You need a full tank of your own energy before you allow others to start to siphon it off. Additionally, your strength and well-being will serve as a model for those who need and require your support.

One of the most common ways we can lose sight of ourselves is in our relationship with a partner, spouse or significant other. Though a successful relationship is based on compromise, it is easy to over compensate in our attempts to meet half way. Before we know it, we are looking and acting like a completely different person. We lose our objectivity and independence because we become submersed in the day-to-day minutiae of trying to be a couple. The important thing to remember is this is not the person your partner fell in love with. The solution here is simpler than you think. In matters of the heart, follow your heart. When you are true to yourself in a relationship, decisions and actions don't require a lot of deciphering or forethought. If following your heart results in your partner running in the opposite direction, then they didn't deserve your heart in the first place.

Love the Perfectly Imperfect You

"We are all wonderful, beautiful wrecks.
That's what connects us--that we're all broken, all beautifully imperfect."

~Emilio Estevez

*A*re you one of those people who dream about finding a genie in a bottle so you could fix everything wrong with your life? Maybe you'd wish to be thinner, or richer, or more confident. Or perhaps you'd ask for your dream job, a stylish apartment, or the perfect relationship. I'm willing to bet that you're not alone in having those daydreams.

Dissatisfaction is something most people have in common. We all have an idea of what our perfect self looks like, and when we see we're not there yet, dissatisfaction sets in. In a way, that can be positive because it pushes us forward and keeps us from stagnation. However, it only works when our goals are grounded in realism and balanced with self-acceptance. If there are unhealthy expectations and a lack of self-esteem, even minor imperfections will get blown out of proportion and become burdens that keep us from ever being content.

Sadly, it is far too easy to fall into this trap. There is a blaring chorus around us that amplifies what our inner voices have been whispering: we are ugly, inferior, and unworthy. Movies, music, and magazines parade before our eyes icons of perfection we can never hope to emulate, while businesses take advantage of our insecurities as a marketing tool. All of these seem to say if we only try a little harder, then we can reach perfection and finally be happy. But that's a losing battle. No matter how hard we try, no matter how far we come, it will simply never be enough to be called perfect.

It's time that we fought against these destructive attitudes. We need to recognize how twisted this thinking is and aim for a healthier frame of mind. So how can we learn to accept ourselves?

First of all, we need to shut off those false messages. Let's evaluate the impact that pop culture has on us and turn away from influences that make us feel bad about ourselves. If you're watching a show that ridicules and shames less-than-flawless physiques, for example, it's time to cut out that habit. The same goes for personal relationships. Time spent with people who are toxic to our self-esteem should be minimized if not eliminated, while supportive and healing relationships must be cherished. It's up to us to decide which voices we listen to.

The next step is to recalibrate our focus. We need to stop obsessing over flaws we can't change and start appreciating our strengths. Instead of worrying over what we can't do, it's time to concentrate on our skills or even step out of our comfort zone and start exploring other possibilities. If you're a lifelong frustrated artist sliding into bitterness, pick up a guitar. If you've neglected your career trying to satisfy a perfectionist partner, it's time to reclaim your self-respect and your future. There's no reason to wallow in self-pity when we can be proactive instead.

Of course, sometimes self-hatred can become so deep and commonplace that it's impossible to fight it alone. In that case, there's no shame in asking for help. Doctors, counselors, and spiritual mentors may all help in the struggle towards self-acceptance.

No matter how far we have to go in learning to love ourselves, it's still more worthwhile than chasing perfection. When we're able to celebrate ourselves for who we are, we are much closer to fulfilling the potential of who we can be. Thus, the journey to becoming our best self is transformed from a fruitless pursuit of impossible ideals into a meaningful process of learning, living, and growth.

Chapter 10

Leave No Regrets

"Don't cry because it's over, smile because it happened."

~Dr. Seuss

Play More – Work Less

"A little nonsense now and then is cherished by the wisest men."
~Roald Dahl, Charlie and the Great Glass Elevator

The advent of the computer age promised shorter working hours and more time to play. As early as 1965, a US Senate subcommittee predicted that by the year 2000 employees would be working only 20 hours per week while enjoying up to seven weeks of vacation annually. However, the opposite has become reality. Today, people are working more hours than ever before. Whether in the office, at the coffee shop, or even on vacation, technology enables us to work anytime, anywhere.

While this does hold benefits in terms of productivity and flexibility, there is a dark side. It often comes with the cumulative price of higher levels of stress, a greater risk of burnout, and the sacrifice of family relationships. In addition, it can rob you of the enjoyment of life.

Learning to enjoy life
People work longer and harder hours, but for what? Without time to actually enjoy life and celebrate relationships, their hard labor is rendered meaningless. Achieving vocational success is pointless if it comes at the expense of enjoying life.

As a society, we must rediscover the joy of play. Instead of being consumed by meeting deadlines and fulfilling expectations, we must carve out time for recreation, for relationships, and for revitalizing activities. Once established, those boundaries must then be protected. Otherwise, all the demands and expectations will press in to reoccupy that space.

In his book, "Choosing to Cheat," Andy Stanley describes our tendency to choose work over relationship. He writes, "Because of our proclivity to veer in the direction of things that stroke our egos, we tend to cheat at home. We give an inordinate amount of our time, energy, and passion to our work." This does not mean that work is evil. Rather, things simply get out of balance when we allow work to take over.

Consider these suggestions for establishing boundaries in your life:

- Spend one or two weeks tracking how you are currently investing your time. What are you doing in your job that you don't have to be doing? Are there tasks that do not need to be completed? Have you assumed responsibilities that rightfully belong to someone else? In other words, what can you eliminate from your "to-do" list?

- Create a template for your typical weekly work schedule. If you have recurring responsibilities, designate a time frame in which they can be completed, while simultaneously honoring the constraints of your job description. For example, if you were hired to work 30 hours, limit your schedule to 30 hours.

- Approach your employer regarding your concerns. If you discover you cannot complete your work within the time allotted, express this to your boss. When you do, consider what suggestions you can offer as alternative solutions.

- Turn off your phone and avoid email when you are "off the clock." Sure, many jobs require that someone be "on call" at all times. If this is true in your situation, take your turn in the rotation. Otherwise, make yourself unavailable after-hours.

- Prioritize your family and friends. Relationships are often the first victims to the constant onslaught of the demands of work. Refuse to allow this to happen in your life. Instead, protect your relationships and devote uninterrupted time toward nurturing them. Let your heart be reflected in your schedule.

- Be willing to walk away. If work is monopolizing your life and if a solution is nowhere to be found, it may be necessary to consider your options. See what other jobs are available for you, even if it means lower wages and accepting a lower standard of living. You are not defined by your title or possessions, so do not cling to them as if you are.

Work is a necessary and beneficial part of living as long as it is kept in perspective. What will it take for you to restore balance between work and play? What safeguards can you put in place to protect those aspects of life that are most important to you? How can you create boundaries to enjoy life to the fullest? By purposefully answering these questions, you can discover pleasure both at and away from the office.

Spend Less - Live More

"Too many people spend money they haven't earned,
to buy things they don't want,
to impress people they don't like."

~*Will Rogers*

Where do you look to find meaning in life? For many people – intentionally or not – the meaning in their lives is wrapped up in their belongings. The more stuff they acquire, the greater their sense of self-worth.

The truth behind material possessions
Do our belongings really reflect our worth, though? Or is our worth measured in more significant ways? The following five concepts can help you gain perspective on how you perceive your possessions.

- True meaning is not measured in terms of belongings, but in terms of family, faith, purpose, and relationships. You cannot evaluate your life by the amount of stuff you have accumulated. It is not about how much you get for yourself; it is about how much you give of yourself.

- You are not defined by your belongings. Your identity is who you are, not what you have. The depth of your character is not measured by the breadth of your belongings.

- Possessions can end up possessing you. When you place

too much value on stuff, your stuff puts you in bondage that ties you to it financially and emotionally. As a result, you become caught up in the continual pursuit for more, while finding yourself trapped in a never-ending quest for the latest toys.

- Wealth cannot buy happiness. Despite the allure of acquiring the latest gadgets in the pursuit of happiness, when you seek material possessions you will invariably come up short. In fact, the opposite effect can become reality. History is riddled with accounts of the rich who find no satisfaction in life. Conversely, the greatest expressions of joy are often evident among the poorest of society.

- Belongings require constant attention. Your stuff will consistently demand more from you, whether you need to repair, update, refurbish, renovate, or replace it. Plus, you must pay for more space to house your ever-expanding collection of belongings. Then you must invest time and energy in regularly tending to them. No, belongings do not bring freedom. Rather, they can be limiting and all-consuming, costing you much more than you originally agreed to pay.

Depending upon your possessions to provide you with freedom and happiness will ultimately disappoint you. Instead, material possession will hold you captive while leaving you dissatisfied with what you have. No matter how much you acquire, you will desire more. On the other hand, intentionally choosing to make do with less is liberating. It relieves the pressure to keep up with the Jones's, empowers you to dig your way out of any indebtedness you may have, and it frees you to become more generous toward others.

Turn a Wish Into a Goal

"Dream as if you will live forever;
Live as if you will die today."

~James Dean

Many of us have wishes we never act upon – wishes we never take steps towards because we're convinced they are only fantasies. We usually think this way because what we desire is so much bigger than what we believe we're worth. Expanding our sense of self-worth allows us to see that our dreams live inside of us for a reason – we are meant to pursue them. Accepting this will put you in a position to turn a wish into a goal.

To turn our wishes into goals we have to first take them seriously. We have to honor our dreams enough to articulate them. "I want an increase in pay." "I want to fit into my old clothes again." "I want to earn money working from home." This accomplishes two purposes: (1) it reaffirms that we feel deserving of whatever change we're trying to make, and (2) it releases energy to help us advance towards the materialization of our wishes.

The difference between a wish and a goal
Anything you dream about will be easier to achieve if you can see it clearly in your mind's eye. Turning a wish into a clearly-stated goal will help you to envision it becoming a reality. Everything we've done in our lives existed first as a thought in our minds. Goals are a kind of middle ground, a journey between an idea and its fulfillment. Before you begin that journey, make sure you

149

know what it is you wish for. Then examine the voices inside you that may be saying your wish is too big or too good for you. It's not necessary we rid ourselves of all such thoughts in order to fulfill our dreams, yet we need to be aware of their existence.

Those detracting thoughts lose much of their power when they're exposed. They're basically saying, "Stay here where it's safe!" When you turn a wish into a goal you expand your life. This can bring up fear. You may be afraid you'll be worse off for having made the leap of faith if you fail, or those close to you may be jealous of your accomplishment should you succeed. Most of us have experienced some version of acting boldly as children when someone bigger than us said, "Who do you think you are?" That sort of voice is often internalized and it can re-emerge whenever we take steps to turn any of our wishes into reality.

Making wishes realities

For this reason, it's wise to be gentle and patient with yourself as you move towards the fulfillment of your dreams. Take some time every day to visualize your wish becoming real. Then make some kind of effort – however small it may seem – to bring that vision into being. What this gesture looks like will vary largely depending upon the nature of your wish. Some general examples could include:

- Smiling at a stranger if you're lonely and longing for companionship.

- Fine tuning your resume if you want a better job.

- Committing to a submission a week if you desire to be a published author.

- Signing up for a gym membership if you want to get in shape.

Such steps get our thoughts and actions moving in the direction of wish fulfillment. Turning a wish into a goal is a matter of clarity, intent and belief. We clarify what we really want, state our intention to achieve it – overriding those "nay-saying" voices inside of us – and then move forward in the full faith that we are the creators of our lives and we can make our own wishes come true.

Embrace the Present

"The secret of health for both mind and body is not to mourn for the past,
nor to worry about the future,
but to live the present moment wisely and earnestly."

~Siddhartha Guatama

Life is a series of moments ranging from memorable and significant to ordinary and mundane. But the fact is all the moments of your life have an impact. It is the little moments that make up a life. To let go of past circumstances, and cease to look only for some future perfect time, is to truly live. If you are thinking about the past, you are living there now. If you are focusing on the future, you are living there as well. Why waste those moments on efforts for no gain.

That does not mean you shouldn't have goals and dreams. Goal-setting has a prominent place in the scheme of things, although we have to remember to live in the now and not let future plans take over current experiences. Have you ever had a moment that seemed insignificant at the time, although it unfolded as a turning point in your life? A fleeting thought, a conversation, or a daily task you had completed many times before; however, something about it was different this time. Something inside you changed in one tiny moment. We often miss points like these. With hearts and minds so full of the past, we leave no space for the gifts offered to us in the present. The great American psychologist Abraham Maslow said "The ability to be in the present moment is a major component of mental wellness." With busy lives, responsibilities, and loved ones depending on us, it can be challenging to stop, inhale, and just be. So how do we do it? How do we live in the now?

Awareness
First up is awareness. Be aware that every moment you live is contributing to the memories you hold, the knowledge you obtain, and the life you experience. There are lessons to be learned when times are good or bad, abundant or lean. Awareness is the ability to consciously feel and perceive what is happening in and around you. It involves self-awareness of your own thoughts and feelings – as well as a sensory perception of the outside world. You can be awake and conscious, yet not actually aware. With a little practice and focus, however, you can learn to be in that higher state.

Appreciation
The next practice we need to adopt in living a life in the present moment is the act of appreciation. The word appreciation has a bit more expansive tone than the word gratitude. The ability to appreciate is being able to recognize pleasure and enjoyment. There are many ways to practice appreciation. Choose one that resonates with you, one that you can easily adopt into your daily life. Here are a few suggestions:

• Take a few minutes every morning before getting out of bed to list a few things for which you are thankful.

• Look daily for the positive aspects of every situation.

• Choose a person in your life you love and come up with a list of things you appreciate about him or her and why.

• Appreciate yourself and all you have accomplished.

• Appreciate every day and watch your life change for the better.

Relationships

Relationships are another important aspect of embracing the present. Friendship and a sense of camaraderie, whether with family, friends, or coworkers, are important to both physical and mental health. Human interaction helps us live in the now by focusing on the wants and needs of ourselves as well as others. Interacting with those around us forces us to reevaluate our own belief systems and refocus on what is happening at present. Adding the previous practice of showing appreciation to family and friends builds happier relationships, while tuning in to the present moment. Take time to share and appreciate the special people in your life every day.

Stillness

This last one – stillness – can be a little harder to accomplish. It is important to take time, even if for a few minutes, to just be. Life is hectic, so quieting the mind can be challenging. Find a quiet place where no one will disturb you and be still and reflect. It does not have to be for a long time - usually taking a few minutes is enough to calm the mind and embrace the present. If you like, you can combine it with the practice of appreciation. Pick something you appreciate and focus on it. Let the reflection wander where it may and see where your mind takes you. It may reveal to you a much needed answer.

Living in the now is an art form, but it does not take hours a day or years in a monastery to master. A few small changes can go a long way towards increasing focus and providing a happier life. Start each day anew with a group of companions, a list of blessings, and time to be completely you.

Epilogue

What I Learned from This Book

As I stated in my Author's Note at the beginning of this book, I believe we are each a work-in-progress. As I researched the material I wanted to include in The No-Regrets Bucket List, I tried to think about how the topics I was exploring related to my personal life. I came to realize becoming the person I want to be is akin to peeling off the layers of an onion. Even after achieving many of my life goals, I realize I have more work to do.

So, in some ways, I may not be qualified to write a book on living a life of no-regrets, as there are areas in my own life that need attention before my death. The realization of the additional work I needed to do became very clear to me as I gathered the material for this book.

On the other hand, I feel in a unique position to write this book for that very same reason. For it is only through an awareness and acknowledgment of what needs to be changed that true change can begin, and it is my desire to share that belief with others.

And so, with a deep sense of humility, I offer this book to the perfectly imperfect human beings each of us are, and to any who might benefit from its reading.

More Blessings,
  Marion Witte

Write Your Own Epitaph

"The highest tribute to the dead is not grief but gratitude."
~Thornton Wilder

*H*ow do you want to be remembered after you are gone? Would you like to be known for how much you loved your family? What about for your devotion to your work. Or is it how you invested in the community. If you could compose a one-sentence summary of the legacy you want to leave behind, what would it say?

Your epitaph is a reflection of you
Your everyday words and actions influence the way you will be remembered for years to come. Indeed, the epitaphs on many tombstones speak volumes of the deceased. Consider these memorable engravings and what they reveal about the dearly departed:

- From an eighteenth-century gravestone in Massachusetts. Obviously, Miss Young had a serious problem with gossip!
Here lies as silent clay
Miss Arabella Young
who on the 21st of May
began to hold her tongue

- The tombstone of a woman known for her critical nature reads:
Here lies my Wife in earthy mold,
Who when she lived did naught but scold.
Good friends go softly in your walking,
Lest she should wake and rise up talking

- William H. Hahn Jr. apparently had a sense of humor as reflected in his tombstone message,

  "I told you I was sick."

- Merv Griffin, the famous entertainer is recognized for his decades in the industry with these final words:

  "I will not be right back after this message."

What would you want your epitaph to say? If you could compose it yourself, what would it say and how would it reflect on you as a person?

Begin composing

Take a moment right now to consider what is truly important to you, then evaluate whether or not it is evident in the way you are living. If giving back to society is important to you, is it manifested in how you spend your time? If your faith is central to who you are, do you live it out in tangible ways? If your children are your pride and joy, are you regularly investing your time and energy into their lives?

Crafting your own epitaph has significant value. It empowers you to intentionally orchestrate your life around it. Instead of living without a sense of purpose, you can establish a clear direction. Rather than wasting your time in meaningless ways, you can purposefully plan and prioritize your schedule. You are then free to direct your most powerful energies toward those things that best reflect your desired legacy.

So what kind of legacy do you want to leave? When you are dead and gone, what do you want others to say about you? If you could inscribe your own tombstone, how would you want to sum up your life?

Of course, "what you want" is not always synonymous with reality. You may have a good idea about how you want to be remembered, but are you building that legacy right now? Everything you say and everything you do—even the attitudes you project—have an impact.

What do you want your epitaph to say about you? Too many people give too little thought toward answering that question, leaving others to compose it after they have passed away. You, however, do not have to leave it until then. Set your direction today, and then begin living according to how you want to be remembered.

I am sharing the epitaph I created for myself, as I believe it reflects the life I want to be known for at this point in time. On the other hand, I am aware that it may change as I grow and evolve.

Here Reclines
Marion Elizabeth Witte

"An Agent of Change"

**She had a Will of Steel
and a Heart of Gold**

Your Tombstone As You Would
Write It Today
(For You to Fill In)

Your Ideal End-of-Life Tombstone

(For You to Create)

Have a Family Member Create
Your Tombstone
(Proceed With Caution!)

Have A Friend Fill In Your Tombstone
(A Good Friend!)

My Personal
No-Regrets Bucket List

This outline provides a starting point to create your own
No-Regrets Bucket List

I am going to discover who I really am by:

_____

_____

_____

I am going to make the following changes in my life:

_____

_____

_____

I am going to learn to:

_____

_____

_____

My daily connection will be:

_____

_____

_____

I will express gratitude by:

_____

_____

_____

I will share myself by:

_____

_____

I will bring more joy into my life by:

_____

_____

I will love more freely by:

_____

_____

I will be true to myself by:

_____

_____

I will make sure I have no regrets by:

_____

_____

Something to Contemplate

Assume that TODAY is the LAST DAY of your life. Complete the following sentence with some action, activity or experience you wish you would have undertaken.

I wish I had

_____

_____

_____

_____

_____

And now fill in the action(s) you are going to take so you don't wind up with that regret(s).

_____

_____

_____

_____

_____

_____

_____

Ideas I Am Going To Explore

Write down the concepts or ideas in this book that interest you, and then search the internet for books or workshops to obtain a more in-depth understanding.

_____

_____

_____

_____

_____

_____

_____

_____

_____

_____

_____

_____

_____

_____

_____

_____

_____

_____

_____

Seven Deadly Sins

1. Wealth without work

2. Pleasure without conscience

3. Science without humanity

4. Knowledge without character

5. Politics without principle

6. Commerce without morality

7. Worship without sacrifice.

~Mahatma Gandhi

The Teachings of Lao Tzu

*These are called attending to great things
at small beginnings*

Tackle difficulties when they are easy.

Accomplish great things when they are small.

Handle what is going to be rough when it is still smooth.

Control what has not yet formed its force.

Deal with a dangerous situation while it is safe.

Manage what is hard while it is soft.

Eliminate what is vicious before it comes destructive.

About the Author

Ms. Witte has an extensive and varied career in the business and entrepreneurial world. She practiced with an international CPA firm and served as the executive vice president for a large tour operator. She has owned and operated a jewelry manufacturing company, computer consulting firm, real estate development company, a CPA firm and a publishing company.

Ms. Witte is an advocate for youth empowerment and educational reform. She founded and manages the *Angel Heart Foundation,* a non-profit organization devoted to supporting parents and encouraging youth. She is also the Editor in Chief of the Foundation's sister websites - *Next Generation Parenting* and *Brave New Leaders.*

Marion recently created *The Wise Woman Collection,* a series of books devoted to education, inspiration and transformation through the sharing of stories and wisdom. She has completed two books in that collection – *Courage of the Soul* and *The No-Regrets Bucket List,* and is working on a third – *Simple Treasures,* a collection of her poetry and illustrations. *Little Madhouse on the Prairie,* her self-help memoir, was published in 2011.

Marion resides in Ventura, California, where she pursues her Foundation, writing and speaking activities.

The No-Regrets Bucket List is part of The Wise Women Collection, a series of books from Wise Owl Publishing, Inc. The books are inspirational and insightful and are based on the following ideas:

Wise Woman Beliefs
The planet desperately needs more peacemakers
and storytellers - Dalai Lama

Wise Woman Offerings
The Wise Woman Collection is a series of books focused on
education, inspiration and transformation through
the sharing of stories and wisdom.

Wise Woman Practices
Tell me and I will forget.
Show me and I will remember.
Involve me and I will understand.

For more information about the Collection, visit
www.wisewomancollection.com

Notes

_____

_____

_____

_____

_____

_____

_____

_____

_____

_____

_____

_____

_____

_____

_____

_____

_____

_____

_____

_____

_____

Notes

CPSIA information can be obtained at www.ICGtesting.com
Printed in the USA
BVOW081626170213

313424BV00003B/3/P